**World
Premier
Hotel Design**

Volume

6

RESTAURANT INTERIOR

Supervision:
Noboru KAWAZOE

Photography & Text:
Hiro KISHIKAWA

KAWADE SHOBO SHINSHA

Introduction

by Noboru Kawazoe

Architectural Critic

The hotel restaurant represents the heart of the hotel and also its public face, and in this volume we will look at new trends in hotel restaurant interior design, and tie up this series of books on 21st-century hotel design.

We once thought of restaurants as being divided into three basic categories—Western, Chinese and Japanese—but restaurants have always been about more than just food, as tableware, furniture, equipment, interior design and the uniforms of the chefs and the service staff all contribute to the restaurant-going experience. Restaurants first came into existence at a time when society was maturing; after the French Revolution there were many unemployed chefs who formerly worked for the royal palace or aristocratic families, and they opened restaurants first in Paris, after which the idea spread to London and other European capitals.

Western Europe in the nineteenth century had many great artists and masters in the fields of literature, music and the fine arts, but there wasn't nearly as much originality in the fields of architecture and industrial arts. It was an era of historicism for both exterior appearance and interior design, with heavy influences from historical styles and other cultures: Greece, Rome, Egypt, the Islamic world, India, China and Japan. This unbalance was also reflected linguistically—painting and sculpture were known as the fine arts, while architecture, interior design and industrial arts were known as the decorative arts. The ostentatious display of this era has been criticized, but looking back at this period when many of the great cities of Western Europe took their present form we can appreciate it as a golden age in the world's cultural history.

By the late nineteenth century there were movements to combine the fine arts with architecture, typified by William Morris and the Arts and Crafts movement and the rise of the Art Nouveau style, and this continued into the twentieth century. After World War I, with the background of mass production of durable goods typified by the automobile assembly line, the French

of living (as we discussed in volume 5 of this series), and he also insisted that he decorative arts of the day were no longer decorative. Taking the place of decoration, we see the birth of conceptual interior design, with abstract designs analogous to the abstract paintings of Picasso and Matisse. Nonetheless, when we look at many of the examples in these books about 21st-century hotel design, we see very noticeable examples of historical interior decoration preserved as is, and newly coordinated with furnishings, curtains and so on. This is one example that demonstrates that we need to take the modern meaning of interior design and analyse it on three different levels—interior design, interior decoration and interior coordination.

The internationalist modern design of the first half of the twentieth century is rarely seen in practice outside of Europe and North America, so it's interesting to examine the real meaning of interior design when we look at "Chinese modern" and "Japanese modern" design where historical interior decorative elements have been removed, for example in modern Chinese restaurants that are stripped of their red-lacquered pillars, lanterns and Oriental screens, or Japanese restaurants with ordinary chair seating. After the Berlin Wall fell in 1989 we can see signs of cuisine moving past the level of ethnicity and folklore, and transcending national boundaries. In particular, when we look at the section of the world stretching from Hawaii to Indonesia, the Pacific region and Southeast Asia, with its abundance of fresh ingredients and multitude of spices, the various ethnic cuisines allow travelers to enjoy a relaxed resort-like experience stripped of the usual hotel formality. Southeast Asia, like China, is also known for its rich street-stall culture. Cuisines like sushi and tempura that are now served in modern hotel settings had their origins as fast food from street stalls, so perhaps we can anticipate new generations of restaurants serving "folk" cuisine following the same path.

Chapter 3 **RESTAURANT INTERIORS IN USA** 142

Printed in China
ISBN978-4-309-80006-6

Chapter 1

RESTAURANT INTERIORS IN ASIA

Glow is the adventurous organic restaurant in The Metropolitan, Bangkok, Thailand.

The Mandarin Pavilion serves contemporary Cantonese cuisine. Shanghai JC Mandarin, China.

Built in the 1990s, the Italian restaurant Grissini was at the forefront of contemporary design. Grand Hyatt Hong Kong, China.
Opposite page: Doc Cheng's serves regional cuisine from Western China and is a newly developed restaurant in the historic Raffles Hotel, Singapore.

Chinese restaurants with Western-style interiors have been a trend in Asian hotels since the early 1990s. A good example of this is One Harbour Road in the Grand Hyatt Hong Kong, the first restaurant we cover in this volume. Avoiding such traditional design elements as Chinese lanterns, red-lacquer columns, Chinese panel screens and traditional ink and brush drawings, the interior here is based instead on a veranda of an old-fashioned mansion belonging to a military official from Hong Kong's colonial past. Design trends do come and go, however, and perhaps now, after 15 years, this particular trend will be gradually giving way to other styles.

One Harbour Road and Doc Cheng's, a restaurant at Raffles Hotel that serves regional cuisine from western China, illustrate some interesting points about Asian hotel restaurants in general: substantial financial resources allow replacement of aging facilities with original cutting-edge interior design, in the process creating restaurants that are very popular with the public. The integration of fresh, modern interior design seems to be an important aspect of their success.

Looked at geographically, the continent of Asia, spanning the distance from Japan to India, is a far bigger territory than the North American continent. Just looking at representative cuisines from China alone, there are distinct cuisines in Canton, Szechuan, Beijing and Shanghai, not to mention smaller individual cuisines from regions near Russia and Korea, incorporating Mongolian and Korean influences, and the cuisines of Western China that are within the cultural sphere of the Arab world. If you add in cuisines from Japan, Indonesia, and the many other countries in the area, it seems like Asia might have the widest range of food cultures in the world.

In addition to well-known national cuisines, each country has its own unique and unusual regional styles of cooking, so there are many chances to discover restaurants with unfamiliar cuisines. Perhaps in the near future the discovery of unusual menus and dishes will be as much a part of the enjoyment of visiting a new hotel restaurant as its interior design.

One Harbour Road

Grand Hyatt Hong Kong
1 Harbour Road, Hong Kong, China
Tel: (852) 2588-1234 Fax: (852) 2802-0677
http://www.hyatt.com

Opening date: 1989
Interior design: Hirsch Bedner & Associates, Hong Kong
Food & beverage facilities: 8
Guest rooms: 572 (including 35 suites)
Contact: Hyatt Hotels & Resorts

In 1995, just before Hong Kong was returned to China, the Hong Kong Convention Exhibition Center opened in a location facing the sea in the Wanchai district of Hong Kong Island. It's an environment bustling with both convention-goers and hotel guests. In contrast with the contemporary mirrored-glass facade, the interior is a mix of Art Deco and contemporary elements, and it is a good example of one type of design popular in today's Grand Hotel. This concept was very influential in the 1990s among Asian hotels. The interior of the Cantonese restaurant One Harbor Road is based on the second-story verandah of a 1930s British colonial mansion on Victoria Peak.

An elevator lobby, seen from a staircase.
Right page: **From the lobby guests ride a special elevator to arrive at this entrance space. There are three dining levels, with waterfalls.**

The hotel building seen from Kowloon. To the right is the Grand Hyatt. The Hong Kong Convention Exhibition Center stands facing the sea.

**Baked crab claws in bouillon with sauteed vegetables;
right: Szechuan-style sauteed scallops with ham and Chinese greens;
Shark's fin soup and braised bamboo and fungi with pigeon egg.**

The two lower levels, seen from the restaurant's best seats. Each level has its own distinctive design and atmosphere.

The presentation plates are from Ginori in Italy. The various plates are done in different designs.

Movable sun visors are attached to the ceiling to protect from the harsh light of the sun.

The ornamental pottery decorating the walls is also by Ginori.

The restaurant's veranda-based design theme can be seen most clearly in the Veranda Room on the second level.

Man Ho

JW Marriott Hotel Hong Kong
Pacific Place, 88 Queensway, Hong Kong, S.A.R. China
Tel: (852) 2810-8366   Fax: (852) 2845-0737
http://www.marriott.com

Opening date: 1989
Interior design: Wong & Ouyang (HK) Ltd.
Renovation date: 1994
Food & beverage facilities: 5
Guest rooms: 604 (including 27 suites)
Contact: Marriott International

This hotel is now part of the Pacific Place complex, which opened five years ago, and includes three hotels, office buildings and an underground shopping mall. When the complex opened, the hotel's guest rooms were upgraded and the dining facilities were renovated. The hotel reopened in 1994 with the JW Marriott brand, a high ranking brand of the Marriott Hotel company.

The Cantonese restaurant Man Ho is decorated in contemporary Chinese style, with a spacious, relaxed dining area. The concept is to provide good food at reasonable prices; the restaurant caters to lunchtime office workers in the Pacific Place complex and also provides tea service.

A gilt Chinese screen panel.

Fish tanks enliven the interior.

A nighttime view of the hotel's facade.

Right page: **The Man Ho dining room features contemporary design; ceilings are painted with gold clouds, and the presentation plates are jade.**

Toscano

The Ritz-Carlton, Hong Kong
3 Connaught Road, Central District, Hong Kong, S.A.R. China
Tel: (852) 2877-6666   Fax: (852) 2877-6778
http://www.ritzcarlton.com

Opening date: 1993
Interior design: Hirsch Bedner & Associates, Hong Kong
Renovation date: 2001
Food & beverage facilities: 6
Guest rooms: 216 (including 48 suites)
Contact: The Ritz-Carlton Hotel Company

This is the Ritz-Carlton's first Hong Kong hotel, situated in the Central district on Hong Kong Island. The second Ritz-Carlton is scheduled to open in 2010.

The main dining room is Toscano, serving northern Italian cuisine, and the interiors show the Ritz-Carlton's characteristic classic-style decor. During the 2001 renovation of the hotel, Toscano's interiors stayed the same. There are plans to adapt Toscano's particular style of contemporary restaurant with a classical interior to new Ritz-Carlton properties opening in various countries around the world.

The Ritz-Carlton logo can be seen on the upper portion of the hotel building.
Right : **Restaurant Toscano is decorated in neo-classical style.**

Petrus has a two-level dining area and offers
a panoramic view of Kowloon.
Right page: **Petrus's dining room is decorated in
late-19th century French style, including three
dome ceilings painted with trompe l'oeil
scenes of clouds in the sky, antique lighting
fixtures and two black marble columns.**

Petrus

Island Shangri-La, Hong Kong
Pacific Place, Supreme Court Road, Central, Hong Kong, China
Tel: (852) 2877-3838   Fax: (852) 2521-8742
http://www.shangri-la.com

Opening date: February 22, 1990
Architect: Wong & Ouyang (HK) Ltd.
Construction company: Dragages et Travaux Public
Interior design: Leese Robertson Freeman Designers Limited
Food & beverage facilities: 10
Guest rooms: 531 rooms, 34 suites
Contact: Shangri-La Hotels and Resorts

This is one of three hotels in Pacific Place, a multi-use
commercial complex on Hong Kong Island. The first
four floors make up the shopping-mall foundation of the
complex, above which rise various buildings including
the three hotels. The Island Shangri-La has a reception
area and dining facilities on the 5th-7th floors, leased
office space on floors 9-38, and guest rooms surrounding
the atrium on floors 39-56. On the top floor, the 56th, is
French restaurant Petrus, named after one of Bordeaux's
finest wines. In the 1990s there was a trend for French
restaurants to return to their classical roots, and the
interior of Petrus is done in classical style.

**The facade of
the fifty three-
story hotel.**

Petrus's private lobby.
Right: **Petrus's private dining room is furnished with a large wine cabinet.**

An antique lighting unit.

The menu covers capture the image of a 1920s restaurant in Paris.

Servingware is by Richard Ginori. Silverware is by Christofle.

Tiffany's New York Bar has a counter and
many box seating areas.
Right page: The bar is decorated with unusual
lighting fixture representing figures wrapped in
gold Egyptian clothing, leather-covered
coach sofas and a stained-glass dome.

Tiffany's New York Bar

InterContinental Grand Stanford Hong Kong
70 Mody Road, Tsimshatsui East, Kowloon, Hong Kong, China
Tel: (852) 2721-5161   Fax: (852) 2732-2233
http://www.ichotelsgroup.com

Opening date: 1981
Renovation date: 1995, 2005
Food & beverage facilities: 8
Guest rooms: 578 rooms (including 25 suites)
Contact: InterContinental Hotels Group

This grand deluxe-level hotel is located in the western
part of the Tsimshatsui district in Kowloon. Tiffany's
New York Bar was newly added during renovation work
in 1995. The concept was to create an elegant bar
without drawing on contemporary Hong Kong design,
and the bar uses Art Deco design to try to recreate the
atmosphere of opulent 1930s New York. The hotel is
owned by Tak How Investment Ltd., a Hong Kong real
estate company that has ten hotel properties, including
some under development, on the American mainland, in
China and elsewhere.

The hotel facade.

Palladio

The Portman Ritz-Carlton, Shanghai
Shanghai Centre, 1376 Nanjing Xi Lu, Shanghai 200040, China
Tel: (86-21) 6279-8888   Fax: (86-21) 6279-8800
http://www.ritzcarlton.com

Opening date: January 1, 1990
Architect: John Portman
Interior design: Bilkey Llinas Design
Renovation date: 1998, 2005
Food & beverage facilities: 7
Guest rooms: 578 rooms (including 68 suites)
Contact: The Ritz-Carlton Hotel Company

Palladio restaurant is named after the famous Italian architect Andrea Palladio (1508–1580). Palladio was an active participant in the 16th-century Italian Renaissance, and the interior reflects this style. It features a tunnel vault decorated with flower-petal-design lights on a coffered ceiling, trefoil arches and a mosaic floor. The restaurant, divided into two separate dining spaces, is equipped to serve couples, groups of ten people, or parties of up to one hundred guests.

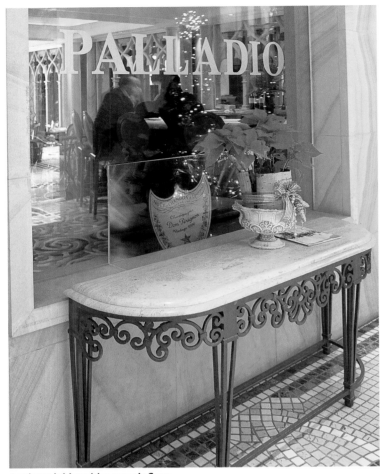

A private lobby with a mosaic floor.

The Portman Ritz-Carlton Shanghai is located in the middle of the Shanghai Centre business complex.

The main dining room includes a window-side private dining area.
Right page:
A passageway between the main dining area and sub-dining area, featuring classical-style trefoil arches decorated with curvilinear tracery.

"One-step" stairs in the middle of the sub-dining room.
Right page: **The sub-dining room set up for a small number of diners. Pizza-making equipment is set up at the front.**

One of Palladio's toilets.

Wine Bar & Grill

Mandarin Pavilion

Shanghai JC Mandarin
1225 Nanjing Xi Lu, Shanghai 200040, China
Tel: (86-21) 6279-1888   Fax: (86-21) 6279-1822
http://www.meritus-hotels.com

Opening date: 1993
Renovation date: 2003
Interior design: John Chan (food and beverage facilities)
Food & beverage facilities: 5
Guest rooms: 600 rooms (including 34 suites)
Contact: Meritus Hotels & Resorts

As part of the 2003 renovation, the Wine Bar & Grill, the Mandarin Pavilion Chinese restaurant and other facilities were built on the hotel's third floor. Hong Kong designer John Chan was responsible for the design of the dining facilities. He is known for creating restaurant and bar designs for a new era, combining a contemporary design sensibility with a more traditional Chinese flavor. In the Wine Bar & Grill, the floors and ceilings incorporate a Chinese design in what is otherwise basically a Western-style design.

The hotel facade.
Right: **The Wine Bar & Grill seen from the entrance. In the back is a bar where a buffet lunch is served, and that is where the restaurant's grill is located.**

Furniture in the Wine Bar is also designed by John Chan.

The dining room of the Mandarin Pavilion Chinese
restaurant is coordinated in contemporary style.
Three private dining rooms are included.

Palace

Peace Hotel, South Wing
20 Nanjing Road (E), Shanghai 200002, China
Tel: (86-21) 6321-6888   Fax: (86-21) 6329-0300
http://www.shanghaipeacehotel.com

Opening date: 1906
Architect: Scott & Carter
Food & beverage facilities: 2
Guest rooms: 103 rooms, 18 suites
Contact: Utell by Pegasus.

The Palace Hotel, which stood next to the Peace Hotel, merged with the Peace Hotel in 1949 and is now the hotel's South Wing. The Shanghai foreign settlement went through four phases of architectural styles between 1850 and the Second World War. The first period was characterized by small Renaissance-style houses with verandas, while larger mansions done in Queen Anne Revival style were popular during the second phase. The third period, during which the Palace Hotel was built, was marked by Neo Baroque-style architecture, and that was followed by Art Deco-style buildings in Shanghai's Bund.

The Palace Chinese restaurant, with its elaborate gilt ceiling cornices, was created from the banquet area of the former Palace Hotel, and it consists of two large dining spaces on different levels. During the 1930s European and American residents of the Shanghai foreign settlement would gather in this space for dances and jazz concerts, and it is an excellent example of the architecture of its day.

To the right is the eleven-story north wing, and to the left the seven-story south wing.

A Palace Hotel poster hangs in a stairwell.

Right page: **The Palace restaurant has unique ceiling cornices and curtain boxes colored in green, red, yellow and pink. Prior to remodeling there was an Art Deco stained-glass dome ceiling. To the left is a separate dining room with its own separate entrance.**

Doc Cheng's

Raffles Hotel
1 Beach Road, Singapore 189673
Tel: (65) 6337-1886 Fax: (65) 6339-7650
http://www.raffleshotel.com

Opening date: April 1887
Main wing opening date: 1899
Architect: R.A.J. Bidwell
Reopening date: September 16, 1991
Interior design: Bent Severin & Associates International
Food & beverage facilities: 15
Guest rooms: 103 (including 18 special suites)
Contact: Raffles International Hotels and Resorts

Doc Cheng's is named after a man who was a pioneer in "medicinal cuisine" and who managed one of the first such restaurants in Singapore, which was located near the hotel. The restaurant here serves food from Hawaii, Asia and the Western regions of China—including dishes like Indochine crab cake, tempura of nori salmon, and tandoor lemongrass chicken—all with contemporary seasonings, portions, and presentation style. Rather than limiting itself to the cuisine of one country, the restaurant serves "trans-ethnic cuisine" covering everything from Western China to Asia. The interior is divided into two parts, with an open-air section done in Colonial style and an air-conditioned section that recreates the exotic ethnic atmosphere of Western China, with its mix of Chinese and Arabic cultural influences.

The original Renaissance-style facade of the main wing has been preserved.
Right: **The open-air section of Doc Cheng's, done in Colonial style.**

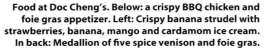

Food at Doc Cheng's. Below: a crispy BBQ chicken and foie gras appetizer. Left: Crispy banana strudel with strawberries, banana, mango and cardamom ice cream. In back: Medallion of five spice venison and foie gras.

Chinese and English writing appears on the presentation plates, mirroring the trans-ethnic character of the cuisine.

A coaster from Doc Cheng's.

The restaurant uses high-backed box seats, helping to recreate the atmosphere of a restaurant in Western China.

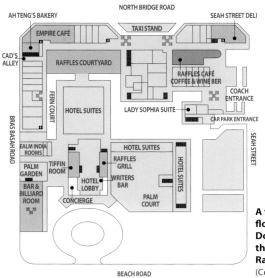

A floor plan of the hotel's first floor and the shopping area. Doc Cheng's is located in the second-floor section of Raffles Cafe to the upper right.
(Courtesy of the Raffles Hotel)

The service staff, dressed in uniforms from Western China.

The Green House

The Ritz-Carlton, Millenia Singapore
7 Raffles Avenue, Singapore 039799
Tel: (65) 6337-8888   Fax: (65) 6338-0001
http://www.ritzcarlton.com

Opening date: January 18, 1996
Construction cost: S$450 million (including site)
Architect: Kevin Roche of KRDJ Associates
Interior design: Hirsch Bedner & Associates, California
Food & beverage facilities: 5
Guest rooms: 610 (including 22 suites)
Contact: The Ritz-Carlton Hotel Company, L.L.C.

Located next to Marina Square, a hotel and under-ground shopping mall complex that was built in the 1980s, the Ritz-Carlton Millenia Singapore hotel is part of Phase Two of the project, costing some twenty million Singapore dollars and consisting of a hotel and two office buildings. The Green House is the all-day dining restaurant, open from early morning to late night and serving Asian, Mediterranean and California cuisine plus pizzas from two pizza ovens. Singapore is a meeting place for many different food cultures, and the Ritz-Carlton, in spite of its world-famous name, decided against having a French restaurant as its main dining room, especially since there are several other French restaurants nearby.

A lunch table setting in the bright atmosphere of the Green House; cake is also served.

The four-story base portion imparts a spacious feel to the hotel facade.

Right page: **A breakfast setting at the Green House, which has 242 seats. Sunlight comes in through the round roof and light is transmitted through hanging tube objects; the glass art on the walls is by Dale Chihuly.**

The front of the two-level lobby lounge, with large glass windows on either side.
Right page: **A view of the spacious lobby lounge, with 28 seats, from the gallery.**

Lobby Lounge

Hotel InterContinental Singapore
80 Middle Road, Singapore 188966
Tel: (65) 6338-7600   Fax: (65) 6338-7366
http://www.ichotelsgroup.com

Opening date: July 19, 1995
Architect: DP Architects
Interior design: Riffanbirg Associates
Food & beverage facilities: 8
Guest rooms: 403 rooms, 56 suites
Contact: InterContinental Hotels Group

This hotel is part of the Bugis Junction development, which is built around a row of recreated traditional shophouses from the Colonial Era, with shops on the ground floor and residential housing above. The lobby lounge is on the first floor of the main wing, and it serves a popular buffet-style high tea. Built in harmony with the surrounding shophouses, the designers opted for Colonial-era decor rather than a more contemporary look.

The facade of the hotel's sixteen-story main wing. There are also 83 guest rooms on the second-floor level of the adjacent shophouses.

The dining area, with large, polished glass windows on one side.
Below the large window is the lobby.
Right page: **Glow's main dining area is marked by iron fence partitions.**

Glow

The Metropolitan, Bangkok
27 South Sathorn Road, Tungmahamek, Shatorn, Bangkok 10120, Thailand
Tel: (66) 2625-3333 Fax: (62) 2625-3300
http://www.lhw.com/metropolitan

Opening date: 2003
Architect: Eco.id Architects and Design Consultancy Pte Ltd.
Interior design: Kathryn Kng, Singapore
Renovation date: 1998 and 2005
Food & beverage facilities: 3
Guest rooms: 171 (including 4 penthouse suites, 1 presidential suite)
Contact: The Leading Hotels of the World

An outdoor pool and part of the hotel facade.
Poolside seating belongs to the restaurant Cy'an.
In back of the wall to the left is the hotel driveway.

In addition to the all-day dining restaurant Cy'an, the hotel also offers the organic restaurant Glow. Amid a worldwide trend in healthy eating, the hotel opened this adventurous restaurant serving only food made from organic ingredients. It quickly became a popular topic of conversation in Bangkok, and there was interest in how Glow would solve the typical problems of an organic restaurant - sourcing a wide enough variety of organic ingredients and keeping prices to a reasonable level. The interior has a simple, contemporary feel, with arrangements of aquatic plants and iron fence partitions coming to symbolize this cutting-edge organic restaurant.

Glow's service staff. The uniform design is by Japanese designer Yoji Yamamoto.

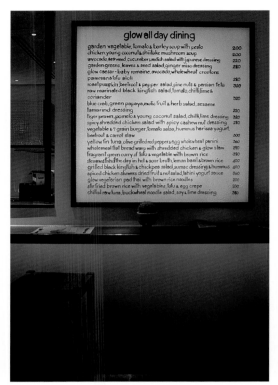

A menu cover at Glow.

A main dish made from seared pink snapper, braised spiced chickpeas, piquillo peppers, sauteed squids, mussels & chorizo.

A dish made from soft-cooked organic eggs, piquillo peppers, caperberries & air-dried tuna.

Glow's main dining area.

Rossini's

Orchid Cafe

Sheraton Grande Sukhumvit Bangkok
250 Sukhumvit Road, Bangkok 10110, Thailand
Tel: (66) 2649-8888   Fax: (66) 2649-8000
http://www.starwoodhotels.com

Opening date: September 1996
Construction cost: US$100 million (including site)
Architect: CASA Company
Interior design: Hirsch Bedner & Associates, Hong Kong
Food & beverage facilities: 7
Guest rooms: 445 (including 25 suites)
Contact: Starwood Hotels & Resorts

This 28-story hotel stands on Sukhumvit Road in one of Bangkok's commercial districts. The Library is a facility offering cocktails, tea, soft drinks and concierge service, but rather than serving as a special executive-floor lounge, it is available to everyone staying at the hotel.

Rossini's restaurant serves southern Italian cuisine. The dining area is divided into two sections by four sliding panels which are covered with trompe-l'oeil paintings. One side shows a typical Italian farm scene, while the opposite side shows shops along the main street of an Italian village; together they help create the atmosphere of the restaurant.

One of the dining areas in Rossini's, featuring a large floral arrangement on the center table. There are sixty seats.

The hotel consists of a five-story public wing facing the street, a 28-story residential tower and a five-story parking facility.

Right page: **Rossini's decor evokes the image of an ancient farmhouse that has been renovated with modern design. On the door is a trompe l'oeil painting of a street with a vault ceiling and a row of columns.**

Rossini's other dining area, decorated with a painting showing a mansion and mountains.

The Orchid Cafe seen from the staircase;
above is the Library.

The all-day dining restaurant
Orchid Cafe has a large circular
buffet table at the center.

The bar area features a semi-circular bar.
Right page: **The dining area has an arched ceiling, which is good for keeping the room cool, and fresco paintings decorate the ceiling.**

Spasso

Grand Hyatt Erawan Bangkok
494 Rajdamri Road, Bangkok 10330, Thailand
Tel: (66) 2254-1234   Fax: (66) 2254-6308
http://www.hyatt.com

Opening date: December 1991
Architect: B & L Architects
Renovation date: 1995
Interior design: Oscar Llinas of Bilkey & Llinas Design
Food & beverage facilities: 11
Guest rooms: 380 rooms, 30 suites
Contact: Hyatt Hotels and Resorts

This site formerly held a large Erawan temple, then a hotel called the Erawan. That rather old hotel was torn down and replaced with the new Grand Hyatt Erawan Bangkok. The hotel's Italian restaurant, Spasso, is divided into three sections, devoted to dining, live music and dancing, and a bar. The hotel is managed by the Hyatt International corporation, which has 215 hotel properties in 43 countries.

The seventeen-story hotel stands on a four-story foundation; the photo shows a view of the facade from the fifth-floor outdoor pool.

The bar area is furnished with
a large round counter. Photos of
famous people from around
the world hang from the walls.

La Scala

The Sukhothai, Bangkok
13/3 South Sathorn Road, Bangkok 10120, Thailand
Tel: (66) 2344-8888 Fax: (62) 2344-8899
http://www.lhw.com/sukhothai

Opening date: November 15, 1991
Architect: Kerry Hill Architects
Renovation date: 2002
Interior design: Design Studio SPIN
Food & beverage facilities: 4
Guest rooms: 104 rooms, 84 suites
Contact: The Leading Hotels of the World

The city of Bangkok has undergone rapid modernization, with rows of tall buildings everywhere you look, so the elegant low-scale spread-out configuration of the Sukhothai makes it stand out from the crowd. The Italian restaurant La Scala was built in 2002, with a contemporary interior decor and several dining areas — an open-kitchen space, a window-side space and an open-air space - that guests can choose from. Interior design is by the Japanese firm Design Studio Spin.

Stupa Buddhist monuments decorate the pool, and the hotel decor incorporates an elegant Sukhothai-dynasty theme.
Right: **A view of the open-kitchen dining area from the window-side dining area.**

Chao Ray occupies its own building in the lagoon.
The tower in the distance is the Sheraton Grande Laguna Phuket.
Right page: **Restaurant Chao Ray's dining area;
to the right is the glass-enclosed kitchen.**

Chao Ray

Sheraton Grande Laguna Phuket
10 Moo 4, Bang Tao Bay, Cherng Talay, Thalang District, Phuket 83110, Thailand
Tel: (66) 76 324 101 7   Fax: (66) 76 324 108
http://www.starwoodhotels.com

Opening date: May 8, 1993
Developers: Tai wa Resort Development Co., Ltd.
Renovation date: 2005
Food & beverage facilities: 10
Guest rooms: 253 rooms, 83 grand villas
Contact: Starwood Hotels & Resorts

This manmade lagoon area includes five international hotels and a golf course; transportation within the lagoon area is provided by free boats. This large-scale development on Thailand's Phuket Island is called Laguna Phuket. The site area is twenty acres, and it is one of the largest such privately developed facilities in Asia. Chao Ray, built in a free-standing building, is a Thai-style seafood restaurant run by the Sheraton Grande Laguna Phuket Hotel. Both hotel guests and outside visitors arrive here by boat. The dining area is next to a hygienic glass-enclosed kitchen, and when the weather permits there is outdoor terrace seating as well. The hotel belongs to Starwood Hotels & Resorts' top-level brand, The Luxury Collection.

Chao Ray also provides Japanese tatami-style seating.

The entrance of Cafe Riviera, which is decorated with large retro-style fresco paintings depicting the era of the Shanghai foreign settlement. In back is the bar.

The Musictheque

Hotel Istana Kuala Lumpur
73, Jalan Raja Chulan, 50200 Kuala Lumpur, Malaysia
Tel: (60) 3 2141-9988   Fax: (60) 3 2144-0111
http://www.hotelistana.com.my

Opening date: August 1992
Architect: Chao Tse Ann
Food & beverage facilities: 6
Guest rooms: 516 (including 64 suites)
Contact: The hotel directly

"Istana" means "palace" in Malaysian, and this Malaysian people's palace is located in the capital city of Kuala Lumpur. The underground Musictheque facility accommodates up to 500 people and was developed with the idea of providing dining and entertainment, with separate bar, disco, theater, cafe and thirteen separate karaoke rooms. Perhaps The Musictheque offers a hint of a future direction in hotel dining facilities, with its unusual theme and design combining food and entertainment.

The hotel's carriageway porch is of Islamic design. The hotel stand on Kuala Lumpur's main road, Jalan Raja Chulan.
Right page: The bar of the underground 1927 Discotheque. The interior design incorporates two themes—the non-stop trans-Atlantic flight of Charles Lindbergh, which was on May 20–21, 1927, and the Art Deco design style that was popular in that era.

Built on the second basement level is Taipan's Club, a reproduction of a 1950s-era Hong Kong bar; the bag to the left was made by Louis Vuitton in the 1930s. Music from the 1950s to the 1970s is played, and patrons can enjoy dancing and dining.

"Malay," one of the thirteen themed karaoke rooms, where food can be ordered. Others include "England" and "Japan." *Right page*: Cafe Riviera is modeled on an Italian terrace restaurant in a Mediterranean port village.

The disco dance floor is decorated with a model of the Spirit of Saint Louis, the plane Charles Lindbergh used for his non-stop trans-Atlantic flight. The airplane propellers are specially ordered decorations made from Murano glass. The chairs are based on designs by Le Corbusier and Josef Hoffmann.

Hors d'œuvres on the buffet table at Spice Market. In another section, raw fish, meat and vegetables are on display, and patrons can order that they be prepared in a particular cooking style.

Spice Market & Lotus Court

Omni Batavia Hotel
Jalan Kali Besar Barat 46, P.O.Box 4922, Jakarta 11049, Indonesia
Tel: (62) 21-782-1051   Fax: (62) 21-782-1051
http://www.omnihotels.com

Opening date: September 28, 1995
Architects: Total Bangal Persada Ltd.
Interior design: David Tey & Associates
Food & beverage facilities: 3
Guest rooms: 391 (including 8 suites)
Contact: The hotel directly

The hotel is located in the Glodok downtown business district of the Kota section of the city, where there remain colorful rows of houses dating back to Dutch colonial days. The famous Batavia name also dates back to colonial days, and the facade of this nine-story hotel is done in the Tempo Doeloe style that was popular in the 1940s. The Spice Market restaurant, lit with numerous small lights and lanterns, strives to create the image of a night market under the starry skies, and serves Asian and international cuisines. Lotus Court has an unusual Chinese-style interior decor and four private dining rooms, and it offers dim sum cart service.

The hotel is located near a harbor where a suspension bridge dating back to colonial days remains.
Right page: **The Spice Market has a hexagonal buffet table in the center, surrounded by the dining area.**

Next Spread: **The Lotus Court has a Chinese-style interior, and serves Cantonese and Szechuan cuisines.**

The Watercourt

Grand Hyatt Bali
P.O.Box 53, Nusa Dua, Bali, Indonesia
Tel: (62) 36-177-1234 Fax: (62) 36-177-2038
http://www.hyatt.com

Opening date: late 1991
Architects: Wimberly, Allison, Tong & Goo
Interior design: Hirsch Bedner & Associates
Environmental design: T. Clarke & Mechler
Food & beverage facilities: 9
Guest rooms: 648 rooms, 41 suites and villas
Contact: Hyatt Hotels and Resorts

This grand-scale resort hotel includes four residential wings, a public wing, six outdoor pools and a 700-meter private beach. The overall area of the grounds is forty acres, and this is the largest in scale of the ten hotels located in Nusa Dua. Development began in late 1989, and twenty months later the hotel opened on April 5, 1991. The development concept was to create a palace of water in elegant Balinese style, and there are waterfalls, ponds and small streams everywhere. The hotel includes lounges, bars, and Japanese, Italian, Balinese, Western and outdoor-stall-type restaurants, so that even guests staying for a full week won't get bored. The Balinese-style Watercourt restaurant is surrounded by a pond, covered with a Balinese-style roof with thick columns and decorated throughout with unique Balinese-style stone carvings to create a relaxed, peaceful atmosphere.

Unique Balinese stone carvings seem to melt into the interior walls.

Balinese stone carvings can also be found at the restaurant entrance, and the staff wear Balinese folk costumes.

The hotel entrance building is also surrounded by ponds and waterfalls.
Right page: seating for the Watercourt restaurant, which occupies a free-standing building. Here the soothing sound of a murmuring stream adds to the healing atmosphere.

Bella Singaraja

Bali InterContinental Resort
Julan Uluwatsu 45, Jimbaran 80361, Bali, Indonesia
Tel: (62) 36-170-1888   Fax: (62) 36-170-1777
http://www.ichotelsgroup.com

Opening date: March 8, 1993
Architect: Hendra Hadiprana
Construction cost: US$150 million
Food & beverage facilities: 8
Guest rooms: 425 rooms, 18 suites, 2 villas
Contact: InterContinental Hotels Group

This large-scale resort hotel stands on an enormous site of 14 hectares located on Jimbaran Beach, 7.2 kilometers south of Bali International Airport. The main wing is built on a pond at the center of the property, and there are also four guest-room wings and a 500-meter private beach. Building plans and interior design were by Indonesian architect Hendra Hadiprana, who used indigenous Balinese building materials to create a design harmonious with its natural setting. On the beach side of the guest wings is the Italian restaurant Bella Singaraja, which has a colonial-era atmosphere and outdoor terrace seating. The simple interior features ceiling fans, wooden floors, plaster walls and rattan chairs.

A view of the rear of the hotel main building from the pond. Several dining and banquet facilities are located there.
Right: A night view of the dining room of Bella Singaraja, with its colonial-era decor.

The buffet table at Bella Singaraja;
meat and fish are prepared by
chefs according to guests' requests.
Right page: **There is an open area in
the middle of Bella Singaraja's
second floor, fashioned after
the second-floor veranda of
a colonial-era mansion.**

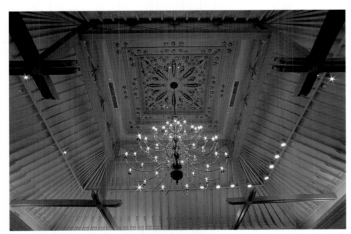

Red, blue and yellow glass panels in the ceiling of
Bella Singaraja create an ever-changing pattern
during the daytime as the sun moves across the sky.

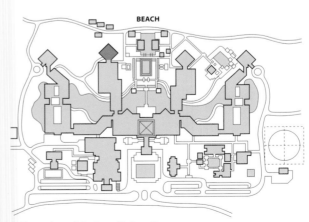

A floor plan of the hotel's first floor.
Bella Singaraja is located at the tip of the second
residential wing along the beach, from the left.
(Courtesy of InterContinental Resort Bali)

The ultra-modern interior of restaurant Hadrian's in The Balmoral, Edinburgh, Scotland.

The interior of Do Leoni restaurant in Hotel Londra Palace in Venice was decorated by Rocco Magnoli, who was also responsible for the Versace boutique.

The service staff of the Michelin three-star restaurant Michel Guerard; Les Pres d'Eugenie–Michel Guerard, Eugenie les Bains, Landes, France.
Opposite page: **The Michelin two-star restaurant d'Hiver is decorated with oak paneling, antique tapestries and a ceiling fresco by painter G. Jaulmes. In the daytime the room is illuminated by natural light from a skylight.**

Chapter 2

RESTAURANT INTERIORS IN EUROPE

European restaurants have a system that helps contribute to improvements in quality—every year in April the Michelin Guide publishes its star ratings for restaurants in France, Belgium, England and other countries. In recent memory the loss of a Michelin star has been a contributing factor for a chef's suicide, and a retiring Michelin editor caused a stir when he revealed some of the internal workings of the rating system. Certainly when a restaurant loses a star it is a very grave matter; Michelin-starred restaurants are often frequented by business executives, and a star loss means fewer customers and less revenue. On the other hand, hotel restaurants will go to great lengths to try to earn a Michelin star, courting Michelin-favored chefs and also those who have been awarded the MOF, a prestigious honor given by the French government. When a restaurant achieves a second Michelin star, it is important news, and a third star is an incredible honor, and will result in non-stop telephone calls for reservations. As of this writing (2006), there are only two restaurants in major European hotels with three Michelin stars. The first is Le Cinq in the Four Seasons George V Paris, and the second is a restaurant introduced in this volume, Le Louis XV Alain Ducasse in the Hotel de Paris in Monaco.

The published criterion for awarding three Michelin stars is to recognize a restaurant that's worth a special journey to visit. Surprisingly, pleasant ambience and attractive decor are not officially recognized as criteria, just the quality of the food. But very few restaurant owners believe this. It is said that in order to receive a third star, more important than innovative cooking are factors like neatly ironed tablecloths and beautiful tableware, appropriate attitude from waiters and service staff, a knowledgeable and helpful sommelier and a well-stocked wine cellar, memorable interior decor and a pleasant atmosphere. So, we find that even if the food is fabulous, if the interior is substandard or the waiters have bad attitude a restaurant won't receive a third Michelin star. Perhaps it is a good thing that this special award for excellence in food culture recognizes these factors. At any rate, it seems that attractive interiors are an important element in European hotel restaurants.

Michelin ★★ 2006

d'Ete & d'Hiver

Hotel Le Bristol
112 rue du Faubourg St.–Honore, 75008 Paris, France
Tel: (33-1) 53-43-43-00   Fax: (33-1) 53-43-43-01
http://www.lhw.com/bristolparis

Opening date: April 1924
Architect: Jammet Ltd.
Renovation date: 1997
Food & beverage facilities: 3
Guest rooms: 134 rooms, 46 suites
Contact: The Leading Hotels of the World

This top-class hotel is located very close to the Palais de l'Elysee, the residence of the French president. One of its special features is its huge courtyard, which gives the impression of a lush green carpet. Located in the courtyard is the popular restaurant d'Ete ("summertime"), which has terrace seating. In the winter d'Ete closes and dining is moved to d'Hiver ("wintertime"). The parents of the hotel's founder ran a restaurant in Dublin, and their son, Hippolyte Jammet, worked at a hotel in Berlin. At the age of 32 he built a hotel in Paris which was owned by his company, Jammet Ltd. He participated actively in running the new Hotel Bristol, working as its manager and director. It opened in 1924, the year before the Paris World's Fair. It was bought by a German hotel management company in 1977. In 1997 it went through a discreet renovation during which it was modernized. This quiet and charming hotel has become a favorite of politicians, diplomats and businessmen.

A seventeenth-century fountain in the garden.
Right page: **The courtyard boasts an area of 1200 square meters. Behind the parasols on the lower left is the indoor dining area of d'Ete.**

The hotel facade is enlivened by a red canopy.

A floor plan of the hotel. When it was first built, there was only the portion of the building surrounding d'Hiver. In 1946 the wing on the right was added, and in 1975 the courtyard and a new wing were added, and the courtyard became the largest courtyard in a luxury hotel in Paris.
(Courtesy of Hotel Le Bristol)

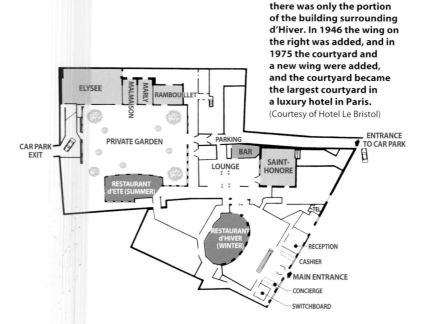

The dining area of the restaurant d'Ete is fashioned after a large tent, and it is air-conditioned.
Terrace seating is outside, on the right.

Chef Eric Frechon started work here in
1981–83, then worked as a sous chef in
the Hotel Byblos Andaluz in Spain, followed
by the three-star La Tour d'Argent in Paris.
In 1988 he became chef at Les Ambassadeurs
at the Hotel de Crillon, and in 1993 he received
France's highest award for a chef, the MOF.
In 1995 he opened his own restaurant,
La Verriere d'Eric Frechon, and in 1999
he took over as chef here.

A breakfast buffet table in "d'Ete."

Outdoor terrace seating at d'Ete. The building on the right was an old monastery, which was restored when the hotel was purchased. Banquet facilities are located on the first floor.

Food at d'Ete. Front row left: A tomato tasting, in aspic, tartar with cucumber and horseradish sorbet, goat cheese on toast. Front row center: lobster casserole-mousseline and fennel braised with vanilla, with herb vinaigrette. Front row right: Roscoff crab in herb aspic, sweet bell pepper jus with lightly spiced anchovies. Center: tender breast of wild duck rubbed with spices, turnip puree caramelized a l'orange, potato souffle. Back row left: rich milk chocolate cream, orange biscuit and marmalade, rum ice cream. Back row right: Iced almond paste calisson, apricot casserole, almond milk jus.

Michelin ★ 2006

L'Espadon

Ritz Paris
15, Place Vendome, 75041 Paris Cedex 01, France
Tel: (33-1) 43-16-30-30   Fax: (33-1) 43-16-36-68
http://www.lhw.com/ritzparis

Construction date: 1704
Opening date: 1898
Architect: C.F. Mewes
Renovation dates: 1988, 1997, 2000
Food & beverage facilities: 4
Guest rooms: 133 rooms, 42 suites
Contact: The Leading Hotels of the World

The plaza and facade were first built in 1688, after the mansion of the Duke of Vendome, which stood on this site, was torn down. The original building of the Ritz Paris main wing was built in 1705 for the daughter of the Duchess of Gramon. In 1896 it was bought by the Ritz Hotel syndicate, and in 1898 it reopened as a hotel. L'Espadon restaurant was opened in 1956 by Charles Ritz, the son of the founder, and although it was open for many years in a different location it returned to the hotel in 1997. The name means "swordfish"; Charles Ritz, who wrote many books on the subject of fishing, was even more famous around the world as a writer and expert on fishing than as the son of the hotel king Cesar Ritz, and the name reflects his passion for the sport.

The Ritz-Escoffier Ecole de Gastronomie Francaise, located in the basement, is named after legendary chef Auguste Escoffier, who worked with Cesar Ritz and was the first chef here. Besides professional courses, the school also offers one-week courses in subjects such as wine knowledge, cheeses, table service, bread and pastries, and general cooking.

The hotel logo, embedded in the ground outside the hotel entrance.
Right: **A special feature of L'Espadon restaurant is the grouping of four sofas and four tables at the center; the dining room is 13.8 x 9 meters and 5.75 meters high, with an area of 124 square meters.**

Trompe l'oeil paintings of sky and clouds decorate the ceiling of L'Espadon.

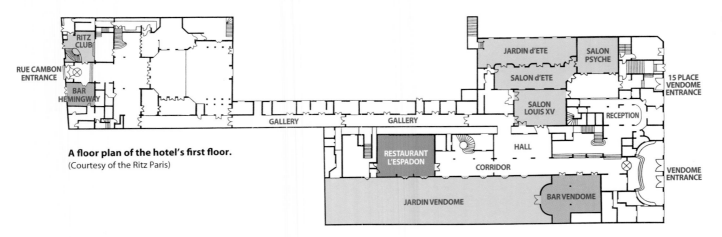

A floor plan of the hotel's first floor.
(Courtesy of the Ritz Paris)

A classroom scene at the Ritz-Escoffier Ecole de Gastronomie Francaise, which has many foreign students.

Terrace seating at L'Espadon, nicknamed the "Vendome courtyard"; at the center is an area where tea is served.

In 1988 the new Ritz Paris opened; before that the entire hotel was renovated, and in the basement level the Ritz-Escoffier Ecole de Gastronomie Francaise, a large pool and the Ritz Club were added. The renovation and reconstruction work cost US$400 million, and goal of its owner, Mohamed Al Fayed, was to restore this to the position of number one hotel in the world. Compared to photos of the original hotel and Cesar Ritz's desires for a simple design, the restoration work is very successful in living up to the hotel's history. The new hotel is very elegant; classical fabrics for interior furnishings have been restored and a range of high-tech conveniences have been discreetly introduced.

A view of Place Vendome from the south. To the left of the Colonne d'Austerlitz, which was built by Napoleon in 1810, is a section of the Ritz Paris marked by a white canopy.

Le Jardin des Cygnes

Hotel Prince de Galles – Paris Champ Elysees
33, Avenue George V, 75008 Paris, France
Tel: (33-1) 53-23-77-77   Fax: (33-1) 53-23-78-78
http://www.starwoodhotels.com

Opening date: 1929
Architect: Arfvidson
Renovation dates: 1984, 2002
Food & beverage facilities: 2
Guest rooms: 170 rooms, 30 suites
Contact: Starwood Hotels & Resorts

This luxury hotel is located just one avenue away from the Champs Elysees, and even today the courtyard retains the original Art Deco design that was very popular in the 1930s. The architect, Arfvidson, decorated the floors, column capitols and walls with mosaics, and he designed a unique patio with an Islamic feel. The courtyard has been restored, and it is now used as the indoor dining area for the restaurant Le Jardin des Cygnes ("the garden of swans"), which is a popular destination for business lunches for executives working in the neighborhood. The hotel's name, Prince de Galles, means "Prince of Wales" and refers to the British crown prince.

Beautiful mosaic patterns decorate
a floor in the courtyard.
Right page: **The mosaic design patio.
Lace curtains hang in the front windows
of the Salon Panache. The photo shows
a view of the upper portion of
the floor plan from the lower portion.**

The hotel facade includes a green canopy.

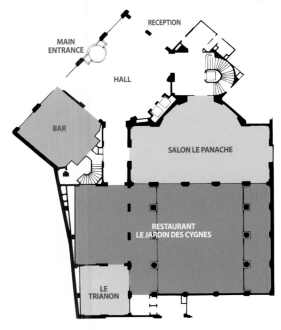

**A floor plan of
the hotel's first floor.**
(Courtesy of
Hotel Prince de Galles)

Chef Pierre Dominique Cecillon has been with hotel for more than twenty years.

Wood plates are laid out in
the center of the patio,
where restaurant seating is located.

Michelin ★★★ 2006

Michel Guerard

Les Pres d'Eugenie – Michel Guerard
40320 Eugenie les Bains, Landes, France
Tel: (33-5) 58-05-05-05   Fax: (33-5) 58-51-10-10
http://www.utell.com

Construction date: 1800s
Opening date: 1972
Food & beverage facilities: 2
Guest rooms: 30 rooms, 10 suites
Contact: Utell by Pegasus

In 1965 a young 33-year-old chef opened the restaurant Pot au Feu in a suburb of Paris. With its excellent food it soon earned a good reputation and attracted an audience of gourmet diners from around the world as well as Parisian celebrities. During the days of Pot au Feu the chef, Michel Guerard, married his talented wife, Christine, who was a graduate of HEC, one of France's top business schools.

In 1972 he moved the restaurant to Eugenie les Bains in the Landes region in southwestern France, and he began serious research toward his goal of creating non-fattening gourmet cuisine. In the 1970s and 80s, in the wake of the worldwide enthusiasm for the nouvelle cuisine movement, Guerard created his own unique healthy version of this cuisine, and in 1977 he was awarded three stars by the Michelin Guide.

The hotel, with its fresh waters flowing from the Pyrenees, clean air, sprawling rustic views, excellent gourmet food and spa waters, is often called a "hotel in heaven."

Chef Michel Guerard and his wife Christine.
Right: **The unusual dining area uses Bisque tiles on the floors, walls and ceiling. The restaurant is divided into three different areas. To the right, a portrait of the Empress Eugenie, a patron of the spa.**

Cuisine from chef Michel Guerard. Left: a gourmet salad. Center: roast duck with green peppercorn sauce. Right: a fruit and sorbet dessert.

2546. EUGÉNIE-les-BAINS (Landes) — Hôtel des Thermes
Coll. J. Lassalle-Calès, Ameublement, St-Sever

The Eugenie spa in around 1850; this is where
the hotel's main wing currently stands.
(Courtesy of Les Pres d'Eugenie – Michel Guerard)
Right page: **The restaurant's backyard dining
area was used as a passageway during the days
when the spa was here. Presentation plates on
the tables are by Villeroy & Boch. Here diners
can enjoy very healthy meals that add up to
only 995 calories per day—270 at breakfast,
370 at lunch, and 365 at dinner—and they can
lose up to five kilograms in a week.**

The menu cover design is
based on a painting hanging
in the restaurant.

La Rotonde

Hotel du Palais
1 Avenue de L'Imperatrice, 64200 Biarritz, France
Tel: (33-5) 59-41-64-00   Fax: (33-5) 59-41-67-99
http://www.lhw.com/dupalais

Construction date: 1854 (as Villa Eugenie)
Opening date: 1905
Architect: Edouard Nierman
Food & beverage facilities: 4
Guest rooms: 132 rooms, 22 suites
Contact: The Leading Hotels of the World

Biarritz, where the hotel is located, is just fifteen minutes by car from the Spanish border. The hotel was originally the Villa Eugenie, used for entertaining European royalty by the Empress Eugenie, the wife of Emperor Napoleon III. As for the origins of La Rotonde, first the Villa Eugenie was damaged by fire. In 1905 it reopened as a casino hotel, and after that it was expanded to include a semi-circular restaurant. During this era it was known as The Grand Dining Room and it featured a beautiful stained-glass skylight. Biarritz is a town with a unique food culture, drawing on influences from French, Spanish and Basque cultures, and it is said to be home to the most beautiful hotel in the world, the Hotel du Palais.

The neo-classic style Hotel du Palais.

Right: **The semi-circular restaurant La Rotonde is decorated in Empire style, and offers a view of the Atlantic Ocean. The design of the iron railing on the lower left incorporates the initials "N" and "E," which stand for "Napoleon" and "Eugenie."**

The facade of the semi-circular restaurant La Rotonde.

Napoleon's initial "N" can be seen at the center of the cylindrical lighting fixtures.

Lighting fixtures decorating the window-side wall in La Rotonde restaurant.

The ceiling of La Rotonde restaurant.

To the left is the entrance hall and to the right is the bar area for La Rotonde; the decor features chandeliers and gilt relief carvings incorporating a design motif related to Napoleon I, including eagles, sphinxes and bees.

The hotel facade was created by architect Edouard Nierman when the building was expanded in 1910. The building to the left of the main wing, known as "La Rotonde" because of its semi-circular plan, was added in 1890. The building on the left is the Grand Casino, built by the same architect who built the opera house in Paris, Charles Garnier.
Right page: Le Louis XV Alain Ducasse is one of only two restaurants in major hotels to have been awarded three Michelin stars (as of 2006).

Michelin ★★★ 2006

Le Louis XV Alain Ducasse

Hotel de Paris
Place du Casino, Monte Carlo, MC 98000 Monaco
Tel: (377) 98-06-30-00   Fax: (377) 98-06-59-13
http://www.lhw.com/deparis

Opening date: 1864
Architect: Godineau de la Bretonnerie
Renovation dates: 1890, 1910
Architect: Edouard Nierman
Food & beverage facilities: 5
Guest rooms: 119 rooms, 72 suites
Contact: The Leading Hotels of the World

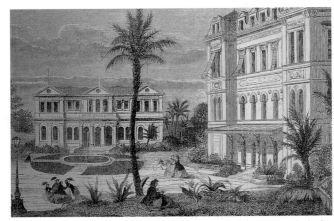

To the right is the original hotel, by architect Godineau de la Bretonnerie, and in front is the casino. After a century of renovations and additions it has reached the scale shown in the photo above. (Courtesy of Hotel de Paris / SBM)

When the tiny country of Monaco gained independence from France 140 years ago, their survival strategy was to build hotels and casinos to create the world's number one resort country. However, Prince Charles III's ambitious plans were not very successful in their execution until Francois Blanc came up with a new idea for a roulette table. His idea was to reduce the number of zero slots in the roulette wheel from two to one, increasing the winning odds for gamblers; when he did this avid gamblers from all over Europe came to Monaco and the casinos made huge profits.

In 1869 the railroad was completed, and European aristocrats, financiers and business leaders came and stayed at the Hotel de Paris. Monte Carlo took its place in the business world, and Monaco indeed became the number one resort in the world. Casinos, hotels, an aquarium, a yacht harbor and golf course were run by the nationally owned SBM (Societe des Bains de Mer), and Monte Carlo also became a leader in F-1 auto racing.

It was here that chef Alain Ducasse, at the age of 32, received his first Michelin three-star rating. A Parisian restaurant under his direction also received three stars, so sometimes he is called the only chef in the world with six Michelin stars. This is known as one of the top hotel restaurants in the world.

The ceiling of restaurant Le Louis XV Alain Ducasse. French artist Marie-Felix Hippolyte Lucas was responsible for the portraits of famous women in French history that decorate the upper portions of the walls and the medallion at the center of the ceiling showing goddesses flying through the sky.
Right page: **The dining room of Le Louis XV Alain Ducasse looks more spacious than it is thanks to the use of numerous mirrors, which date from the original 1910 construction. The window-side mirrors are decorated with classical scenery, and to the left is a portrait of Madame de Pompadour.**

Sauteed red mullet with new potatoes.

A salad of seasonal vegetables with truffles.

An entrance seating area for the restaurant.

A portrait of King Louis XV's love, Madame de Pompadour, hangs in the restaurant entrance area.

An antique French barometer from the 19th century. On the right page is an antique French longcase clock.

Small stools called tabourets sit between chairs and can be used for placing ladies' handbags.

This world-class restaurant has pillars decorated ostentatiously with onyx. The armchairs are Cabriolet Louis XV fauteuil antiques, the servingware is "decor inalterable" Limoges china by Berbardaud, and the glasses, marked with the initial "L" for Louis XV, are by Christofle.

Axelstuberl

Steigenberger Axelmannstein
Saizburger Strasse 2-6, 83435 Bad Reichenhall, Germany
Tel: (49) 8651-7770 Fax: (49) 8651-5932
http://www.worldhotelsgroup.com

Opening date: 1909
Renovation dates: 1971, 1997-98
Food & beverage facilities: 3
Guest rooms: 156 (including 8 suites, 5 apartments)
Contact: Worldhotels

This is one of the finest hotels in Bad Reichenhall, which was originally built as a castle block during the Roman Empire and became well known as a spa resort in the 19th century. The town had many treatment facilities using mineral-salt baths and salt water for drinking, and it drew guests from as far away as North America in the 1930s.

In 1971 the hotel added an indoor pool and a medical facility wing with mineral-salt treatments. In 1997 an Aslan therapy spa facility opened, and in 1998 the main wing and the dining facilities were renovated. Next to the main entrance is a separate entrance for the low-calorie restaurant Axelstuberl. Unlike the modern design of the Park Restaurant main dining room, Axelstuberl's interior reflects an earlier era when community cafes flourished in the mountains.

The back of the hotel's main wing; in the distance are the German Alps. The city of Salzburg in Austria is twenty minutes away by car.
Right: The entrance area of Axelstuberl. The interior design, with its big fireplace and pine-paneled walls and ceiling, is typical of the German southern Alps region.

Axelstuberl's second dining room.

Agnes

Hotel Casa Marcello
Pasnovka 783, 11000 Praha 1, Czech Republic
Tel: (420) 222-311-230   Fax: (420) 222-313-323
http://www.concordehotels.com

Construction date: *c.* 1250
Opening date: September 1995
Food & beverage facilities: 1
Guest rooms: 20 (including 12 suite apartments)
Contact: Concorde Hotels

Hotel Case Marcello, with its historical roots in a 700-year-old monastery, is a small hotel just three minutes from Prague's old city center. In 1253 Prague's first Gothic-style church was built, and it was used as a monastery by the Dominican order for 300 years. In the nineteenth century a portion was purchased by the Italian nobleman Don Marcello, and it has been owned by his family, for whom it is named, until recently. Agnes restaurant occupies part of the ground floor arch foundation of the four-story structure, and the interior is decorated with plasterwork in the original medieval style. A fresco painting dating back to the opening of the monastery has been preserved, and there is a lounge where afternoon tea is served.

The four-story hotel is connected to a residential district dating back to ancient times.

The chef and service staff.

Right: **The original foundation arch is used as is in Agnes's main dining room.**

Hradcany

Hotel Savoy
Keplerova 6, 11800 Praha 1, Czech Republic
Tel: (420) 224-302-430 Fax: (420) 224-301-128
http://www.lhw.com/savoyprague

Opening date: 1907
Architect: J. Verich
Reopening date: 1997
Food & beverage facilities: 3
Guest rooms: 55 rooms, 6 suites
Contact: The Leading Hotels of the World

The Hotel Savoy is a compact, elegant boutique hotel standing on Keplerova street near the entrance to Praha Castle. The building, originally built at the beginning of the nineteenth century, was renovated and the original Hotel Savoy was reopened with Austrian investment money after the democratization of the Czech Republic. The Hradcany restaurant has an unusual electrically powered glass ceiling that opens and closes, allowing fresh air in the warmer months and a view of the starry sky at night. This modern restaurant is the only one of its kind in Prague. The restaurant Hradcany, serving Czech and Continental cuisine, presents a different face at breakfast, lunch, and dinnertime.

Separated a bit from the center of town, the restaurant is at the same level as Prague castle. The bright wall in the center is the hotel facade. The building has five stories above ground and one below.
Right: **Restaurant Hradcany has 75 seats, and outside the electrically operated ceiling is a covering to protect against strong winds. Lights are set within the plants decorating the upper portions of the columns.**

Sarah Bernhardt

Hotel Pariz
U Obecniho domu 1, 11000 Praha 1, Czech Republic
Tel: (420) 222-195-195   Fax: (420) 224-225-475
http://www.concordehotels.com

Opening date: 1904
Architect: Jan Verich
Interior design: A. Pfeifer
Interior design: J. Coler
Reopening date: 1997
Food & beverage facilities: 2
Guest rooms: 95 (including 47 suites)
Contact: Concorde Hotels

This boutique hotel stands next to the Municipal House (Obecni Dum) where Smetany Hall, the venue where Praha's international music festival is held every spring, is located. It was bought in 1923 by the Brandejs family, who were in the hotel business, then it was taken over by the government during the years of communist rule, and it was returned to its original owners in 1991. The building was completely renovated, its original Art Nouveau design was restored, and it reopened for business in 1997.

Sarah Bernhardt restaurant is attached to Gatsby's Bar, and patrons first meet in the bar area and then are shown to their seats in the dining room. The restaurant is named after "European songstress" Sarah Bernhardt, who stayed at the hotel. It is said that when she stayed here massive crowds of her fans gathered outside to catch a glimpse of her traveling between the hotel and the nearby Smetany Hall for her performances.

The impressive facade shows a unique mix of **neo-Gothic and Art Nouveau design.**
Right: **Restaurant Sarah Bernhardt acquired a new ambience during the 1997 renovation. The original restaurant had a larger Art Nouveau-style chandelier. The restaurant, behind the right-hand pillar of Gatsby's Bar, serves French and Czech cuisine.**

The chandelier in the restaurant's entrance was made in 1997.

A portrait of Sarah Bernhardt on the menu cover, by Art Nouveau poster artist Alfons Musha.

The original gilt mosaic design of the walls and pillars has been preserved.

A hotel sign marking the entrance to the Art Nouveau-style cafe.

The unique small chandelier hanging from the upper portion of the restaurant's mirrored pillar. The Art Nouveau-style chandelier dates back to the 1997 renovation.

Bottom row left: Marinated prawns on herbs with octopus and steamed beans. Bottom row center: Stuffed trout with potatoes and steamed vegetables. Bottom row right: Lobster soup with cinnamon. Bottom row far right: Yogurt mousse with blueberries and strawberries on vanilla ice cream. Middle row left: Fruit cake with strawberries and pears. Middle row center: Venison terrine of quail stuffed with plum sauce and cranberries. Middle row right: Lamb chop with rosemary oil and paprika sauce. Top row left: Roast duck breast with peaches, vegetables and chicken liver. Top row center: Chocolate mouse with nougat on strawberry-vanilla ice cream. Top row right: Duck liver parfait with sliced truffles and orange jelly.

Corso

Hotel Bristol, Wien
Kaemtner Ring 1, A-1015 Wien, Austria
Tel: (43-1) 51-51-60   Fax: (43-1) 51-51-65-50
http://www.starwoodhotels.com

Opening date: 1892
Reopening date: 1905
Architect: Edouard Nierman
Food & beverage facilities: 3
Guest rooms: 142 (including 10 suites)
Contact: Starwood Hotels and Resorts

The famous Hotel Bristol stands next to the Staatsoper (State Opera House). Two years after it opened it was purchased by business entrepreneur Karl Wolf, who expanded it, and at the beginning of the twentieth century it was known as the place where world-famous musicians like Toscanini stayed when they were in town. Even today it is one of the main hotels where music-lovers stay when they visit the music-oriented city of Wien. And restaurant Corso is known as an indispensable restaurant that serves post-performance dinners until 1am to patrons of the Opera House.

The classical spiral-columned fireplace is the restaurant's symbol.
Right page: **Corso is a popular spot for late-night dinners after performances at the Opera House next door. The classical design of the interior helps maintain the opera-going mood.**

To the left is the State Opera House, to the right the Hotel Bristol. The hotel has an ideal location for foreign visitors to the Opera House.
(Courtesy of Hotel Bristol, Wien)

Hotel Bristol faces the main Ringstrasse street in Wien.

The riverside hotel. In back is the Mozart Museum.

Zirbelzimmer

Hotel Sacher Salzburg
Shwarzstrasse 5-7, A-5020 Salzburg, Austria
Tel: (43-662) 88-977-0   Fax: (43-662) 88-977-551
http://www.lhw.com/sachersal

Opening date: 1866
Renovation date: 2001
Architect: Baron C. Schwartz
Food & beverage facilities: 5
Guest rooms: 113 rooms, 3 suites
Contact: The Leading Hotels of the World

This famous hotel is one of the finest in Salzburg. With its ideal location on the banks of the Salzach River, the hotel offers views of the castle and the old town. Since being used by Richard Strauss and other founders of the original Salzburg Music Festival, which began on August 22, 1920, the hotel has accommodated festival-goers and staff each year during festival season (mid-July to late August), as well as serving as the bustling center for the social scene surrounding the event.

Of the dining facilities, Cafe Sacher is very popular with the local community. Salzachgrill serves local Salzburg specialties. There is also a Confiserie, under the same management as the cafe selling Wien's famous sacher torte. And Zirbelzimmer restaurant, decorated in the style of a local mountain cabin, is known for its outstanding game-bird dishes, and is popular with foreign visitors.

The chef and service staff.
Right page: **The interior design of Zirbelzimmer restaurant is based on that of a typical Austrian mountain cabin, and it is decorated with deer antlers, pottery and folk musical instruments.**

Next Spread: **A panoramic view of Zirbelzimmer; in front is a breakfast restaurant.**

The River

The Savoy—A Fairmont Hotel
Strand London WC2R 0EU, England, UK
Tel: (44-20) 7836 4343   Fax: (44-20) 7240 6040
http://www.fairmont.com

Opening date: 1889
Architect: T.E. Collcutt
Renovation date: 2001
Food & beverage facilities: 5
Guest rooms: 207 rooms, 48 suites
Contact: Fairmont Hotels & Resorts

When the Savoy Hotel opened a century ago it broke all the rules of stiff Victorian-era society. And in London's social circles it became known as the premier place to dine.

This grand-scale hotel was one of the first places in London where electric lights run by a private generator glittered inside and out, and when the Savoy Restaurant opened it took the lead as a place where people could enjoy a late dinner after the theater, and where women could dine by themselves without male accompaniment. These daring innovations were the idea of the hotel's general manager Cesar Ritz, who was later known as the "King of Hotels." Backing him up was the legendary chef Auguste Escoffier, and together they were a formidable team. Their biggest supporter was the Duke of Windsor, later to become King Edward VIII. The hotel, thanks to Ritz and the support of the crown prince, became a force that helped change London society, and today the Savoy Hotel can be seen as a showcase for the origins of the modern grand hotel.

After renovation, The River restaurant in its present-day form.
Right page: **The Balcony seats in The River restaurant are popular at breakfast. This area was a balcony without windows when it opened in 1889.**

The River restaurant before its 1998 renovation.

A view of the back of the nine-story hotel main wing from the Thames River walkway. Originally the guest rooms had balconies and there were small towers in the two upper corners.

Richard D'Oyly Carte, the hotel's founder, hired Cesar Ritz as hotel general manager and allowed him his innovative policies. D'Oyly Carte was known as a connoisseur of his day; he was an entrepreneur, and he also owned the Savoy Theatre next to the hotel. Around the beginning of the 1880s he crossed the Atlantic and took a tour of the United States that held many surprises. In Chicago the streets were brightly lit at night with electric streetlights, and the large-scale hotel where he stayed had telephones and electric elevators powered by a private generator. He crossed the rest of the continent by railway to San Francisco, and there he stayed at the brand-new Palace Hotel, one of the biggest hotels in the world. There he formed his plan to build the first large-scale hotel in a newly modernized London.

At the time there were no London hotels where the staff treated guests equally regardless of social status or where women could dine alone, and these were two of D'Oyly Carte's goals when he returned to London and built the Savoy Hotel, equipped with all the latest American-style conveniences. He had other ambitions as well, and one goal was to target the rich Americans who crossed the Atlantic on the beautiful ocean liners of the time, and this was the impetus for the creation of the American Bar in the hotel. A century ago the spirit of D'Oyly Carte's ambitious project helped change the times he lived in. What should we expect of the Savoy in the 21st century?

Portraits of American movie stars hang from the walls of The American Bar; there is also a bar counter area.

An illustration of the original lobby. During the 2001 renovation the design of the entranceway, columns, ceiling and other elements was based on this illustration.
(Illustration courtesy of The Savoy)

Afternoon tea in the Thames Foyer. *Right page*: **The original design has been preserved in the Thames Foyer, which serves afternoon tea. The floor is designed to allow dancing, and today jacket and tie are no longer required. In the far corner is the River Restaurant.**

Hadrian's

The Balmoral
1 Princes Street, Edinburgh EH2 2EQ, Scotland, UK
Tel: (44-131) 556-2414   Fax: (44-131) 557-8740
http://www.lhw.com/balmoral

Opening date: 1902
Architects: Beattie & Scott
Renovation date: 1988–1991
Food & beverage facilities: 4
Guest rooms: 188 (including 20 suites)
Contact: The Leading Hotels of the World

The Balmoral hotel, a station hotel with a distinctive clock tower located on Edinburgh's main thoroughfare, has symbolized the city of Edinburgh since its opening days. In 2001 the hotel underwent a complete renovation, at which time the guest rooms and dining facilities were transformed beyond recognition.

Hadrian's is a chic brasserie with a contemporary interior and a separate bar area. Perhaps this illustrates the benefits of renovating and modernizing the interior of an old hotel.

While the style of this hotel, just upstairs from the station platform, has been preserved, the interior has been renovated to create a contemporary feel.
Right: Hadrian's contemporary interior design features walls with pea-green wallpaper and objets d'art, Oriental-style lighting fixtures, and polished-glass servingware.

La Piazzette De La Ville

InterContinental Rome
Via Sistina 67/69 Rome 00187, Italy
Tel: (39) 06-67331   Fax: (39) 06-6784213
http://www.ichotelsgroup.com

Opening date: 1925
Architect: Joseff Vargo
Renovation date: 1994
Food & beverage facilities: 2
Guest rooms: 192 (including 33 suites)
Contact: InterContinental Hotels Group

This hotel is located next to Rome's famous Spanish Steps. The eighteenth-century building was renovated by Hungarian architect Joseff Vargo in 1925 after which it opened as a hotel. Later, the building behind the main wing was purchased and after a number of further renovations we have the present-day hotel. During the 1994 renovation the interior of the restaurant La Piazzetta De La Ville (the name means "a small courtyard") was decorated in a muted color scheme while preserving its classical atmosphere. There is also a separate area on the window side that is decorated in a different color scheme and accented with Ionic columns. The fabric on the backs of the chairs is designed to match the striped pattern of the marble floors, and the plates are decorated in a black-and-white Madeira pattern; similar lines and patterns in these colors can be seen throughout the interior.

The hotel is located on the Via Sistina;
the obelisk in front is at the Spanish Steps.
Right: The round pillars in La Piazzetta De La Ville
restaurant are painted to resemble stone using
a technique known as scagliola.

A nineteenth-century antique mirror.

A chandelier of Murano glass.

The Villeroy & Boch presentation plates have a marble pattern.

Classical-style curtains.

The interior of
La Rotonde restaurant,
used for group
breakfasts,
is surrounded by
round columns.

A pathway leading to
the annex from the
main wing.
To the left and right of
the statue are men's and
women's public toilets.

The second-floor gallery of Il Fiolio is used as a breakfast restaurant.

Il Fiolio

Grand Hotel, Firenze
Piazza Ognissanti 1, Firenze 50123, Italy
Tel: (39-55) 27161   Fax: (39-55) 217400
http://www.starwoodhotels.com

Construction date: 17th century
Architect: Fillipo Brunelleschi
Opening date: 1890
Reopening date: 1990
Food & beverage facilities: 3
Guest rooms: 94 rooms, 13 suites
Contact: Starwood Hotels & Resorts

This hotel in Ognissanti Plaza on the Arno River and The Westin Hotel Excelsior, Firenze, which directly faces it, are sister hotels. The building was originally built by the famous architect Filippo Brunelleschi and was used as a mansion by the Giuntini family. It was remodeled in 1890, after which it opened as the Grand Hotel Royal De La Paix. At the time many Englishmen stayed at the hotel, and it was also known as Continental Hotel Royal De La Paix. Ciga Hotels purchased the hotel in 1957 and managed it for many years, then it was closed between 1974 and 1986. It underwent large-scale renovation and restoration work, during which the Giardino d'Inverno ("winter garden"), a multi-purpose courtyard restaurant and bar, was added. The hotel reopened in 1990.

A view of the Grand Hotel, Firenze, from The Westin Hotel Excelsior. To the left is the Arno River.
Right page: **Giardino d'Inverno is also used for wedding receptions; it is 300 square meters in size and can accommodate 300 persons for banquet-style events. The bar is on the left and the dining room on the right.**

Il Fiolio Bar is a chic, tiny bar with only eight seats.

Before Il Fiolio was built, the glass-ceilinged courtyard, called the "Winter Garden", was the location of the hotel restaurant, and it had a Spanish-style fountain at its center. Around 1890 these glass-ceilinged facilities were very fashionable in European hotels, and many of them had names similar to "Winter Garden." In them guests could enjoy meals and tea service in a warm greenhouse-like space even in mid-winter.
(Courtesy of Grand Hotel, Firenze)
Right page: **The first-floor space of Il Fiolio restaurant has only eight tables.**

A floor plan of the ground floor of the present-day hotel. The gray portion is private residences; the multi-purpose building houses both the hotel and private residential housing.
(Courtesy of Grand Hotel, Firenze)

LUNGARNO A. VESPUCCI

PIAZZA OGNISSANTI

MAIN ENTRANCE

HALL

RECEPTION HALL

GIARDINO d'INVERNO

SALA MONTEBELLO 1

SALA MONTEBELLO 2

SALA MONTEBELLO 3

VIA MONTEBELLO

ENTRANCE

Le Marocain

La Mamounia
Avenue Bab Jdid, Marrakech, Morocco
Tel: (212-44) 38-86-00   Fax: (212-44) 44-49-40
http://www.lhw.com/lamamounia

Opening date: 1923
Architects: A. Marchisio & Henri Prost
Renovation date: 1953, 1977
Food & beverage facilities: 11
Guest rooms: 171 rooms, 56 suites, 3 villas
Contact: The Leading Hotels of the World

This hotel, originally built and managed by the state-run railway company during the French colonial era, is now known around the world as a casino resort hotel. It was designed by French architects A. Marchisio & Henri Prost. The three-story building has 100 guest rooms and the design is a mix of traditional Moorish Arab style and Art Deco style, with a unique interior that was designed to create an exotic, adventurous setting for foreign guests. In 1953 a five-story annex and a casino were added. During the 1992 renovation the traditional restaurant Le Marocain was restored. The floors and walls are decorated with Zelliges-style mosaic tilework, the upper portions of the pillars are decorated with hand-colored carved wood in a design called Muqarnas, and the colorful ceiling is made from Himalayan cedar. The restaurant serves traditional Moroccan cuisine, prepared by female chefs, as is the local custom. There are performances of traditional folk dancing during dinner.

The guest-room wing, remodeled in 1992. The area on the left with the parasols is the restaurant Les Trois Palmiers ("three palm trees"), where guests can enjoy breakfast in the fresh morning breeze.
Right: **The design of Le Marocain restaurant is fashioned after an arbor at the end of a long corridor in a Moroccan palace.**

Ceiling decorations in Le Marocain. The ceiling is made from Himalayan cedar, and the upper portions of the walls are painted wood carvings.
Right page: The central area of Le Marocain. The low-backed seats are a unique Moroccan design; they are provided for foreign visitors who are not used to sitting on the floor. The floor is decorated with mosaic tiles.

This special dining room in Le Marocain has an octagonal dining area surrounding a fountain. During the renovation pillars were replaced by mirrors.

Chapter 3

RESTAURANT INTERIORS IN USA

Pacific Rim cuisine at the Coast Grill restaurant;
Hapuna Beach Prince Hotel, Hawaii Island, Hawaii, USA.

Ceiling lighting at Asiate; below are Asian-style
wood screens and fabric-covered walls at Mobar.
Mandarin Oriental New York, New York, NY, USA.
Opposite page: **New York's newest hotel restaurant, Asiate.
The 21st-floor panoramic view of Central Park is part of
its charm. Mandarin Oriental New York, New York, NY, USA.**

In the mid-1990s a new boom in cuisine in the US started not on the mainland but in Hawaii. With roots in traditional Hawaiian cooking, this new cuisine became hugely popular. Called "Pacific Rim" cuisine, it incorporated dishes from Mexico, Japan, China, Vietnam and India, presented artfully with many small dishes in the style of Japanese kaiseki, and for mainland tourists visiting Hawaii who were unfamiliar with Asian cuisines it was a very impressive experience. Programs featuring popular Pacific Rim restaurants were broadcast regularly on Hawaiian television and attracted large audiences. Thanks to a combination of artful presentation of the food, fresh new menus with a resort feeling, and the success of an ingenious PR campaign, this style has now become standard Hawaiian cuisine.

At the opposite end of the country, New York was at the cutting edge of trends in hotel restaurants during that period. Looking back at 1995 shows us some surprising things. Lespinasse restaurant at The St. Regis Hotel was extremely popular, with three dinner seatings per night, thanks largely to the restaurant's innovative cooking style which incorporated Asian spices into French cuisine.

Moving forward to the spring of 2006, let's look at the famous experimental restaurant at the Hotel Mandarin Oriental New York. The restaurant Asiate, located on the 21st floor of an eighty-story skyscraper, has an interior by Asian designer Tony Chi. He has created an unusual, unique space in this design-focused hotel. The French-Japanese cuisine is also out of the ordinary, and today the restaurant is so popular that it is hard to get reservations. Creating a restaurant on the basis of new ideas alone is representative of the power of America's pioneering spirit, and perhaps also a necessity in the world of New York hotel restaurants, which is dynamic, quickly evolving and fiercely competitive.

A view of the Garden Court from the second-floor banquet facilities.
Right page: **The Garden Court restaurant, renovated in 1991, has 176 seats. The lounge area at the entrance has 88 seats.**

Garden Court

Palace Hotel
2 New Montgomery Street, San Francisco, California 94105, USA
Tel: (1-415) 512-1111   Fax: (1-415) 543-0671
http://www.starwoodhotels.com

Opening date: October 2, 1875
Architect: J.P. Gaynor
Reconstruction date: 1909
Architects (reconstruction):
Trowbridge & Livingstone, George Kelham
Food & beverage facilities: 4
Guest rooms: 551 rooms, 30 suites
Contact: Starwood Hotels & Resorts

This was one of the first large-scale hotels to be built, and the first in the world with such modern conveniences as electric lights, elevators and heating and cooling systems. It was renovated in 1991 by the architecture firm of Skidmore, Owings and Merrill, who completely transformed the entire interior and added an indoor swimming pool.

The Garden Court restaurant, which first opened in 1909, was also restored to its original radiance. Three meals per day plus afternoon tea are served here, in what was originally described as the world's most beautiful glass-domed restaurant.

The hotel's exterior, on New Montgomery Street.

A portion of a decorative frame in the glass-domed ceiling. Some 70,000 pieces of stained glass were replaced by a specialized team of ten workmen, and the entire cost of the restoration work was $7 million.

Small lanterns hang between Corinthian columns, supplementing the light from the Garden Court's large chandelier.

Classic-style candelabra-style lighting fixtures located between wall pillars; originally fixtures of this type held candles.

Window sections built between the vertical frames of the glass dome; the overall design resembles bay windows on a roof.

Right page: **Garden Court seen from the front entrance; afternoon tea is served in the center table area.**

The Dining Room

The Beverly Wilshire
9500 Wilshire Boulevard, Beverly Hills, California 90212, USA
Tel: (1-310) 275-5200   Fax: (1-310) 274-2851
http://www.lhw.com/regbevwils

Opening date: January 1, 1928
Developer: Walter G. McCarty
Architects, designers: Walker & Eisen
Renovation date: 1998
Interior design: Hirsch Bedner & Associates
Food & beverage facilities: 3
Guest rooms: 395 (including 120 suites)
Contact: The Leading Hotels of the World

This hotel was originally called the Beverly Wilshire Apartment Hotel, and it was built as part of the redevelopment project in which the area around the Beverly Auto Speedway was replaced by an upscale residential district. The opening ceremony, on New Year's Eve, 1927, was said to be a lavish affair in which some 400 neighbors were invited to an eight-course dinner. In 1971 the Wilshire Wing was added in back, and the hotel took its present name. Through its history its guestbook has been signed by numerous Hollywood stars and members of royalty from around the world. The hotel underwent renovation work in 1989 and 1998 during which the entire interior was transformed into the modern hotel it is today.

The Dining Room is known for its elegant, modern interior fabrics, and even today it is famous as a gathering spot for Hollywood stars and film-industry people.

The facade of the E-shaped Beverly Wing, which faces Wilshire Boulevard. The original Italian Renaissance-style design has been preserved, and beautiful relief carvings can be seen on the first-floor exterior.
Right: **The Dining Room serves California and Continental cuisines. A trompe l'oeil fresco painting of clouds in the sky decorates the ceiling in this dignified setting that has been popular with Hollywood celebrities for nearly a century.**

Before the 1989 renovation this was El Padrino restaurant.

The presentation plates are Murano glass.

The colorful flower arrangements at the center of the Dining Room embody Hollywood style. The chandelier hanging from the fresco-painted ceiling is Murano glass, the wall pillars are made from mahogany, and the walls are paneled in satinwood. Traditional Italian paintings hang from the walls.

The Grand Cafe serves
only breakfast and lunch.

Grand Cafe

Omni Los Angeles Hotel at California Plaza
251 South Olive Street, Los Angeles, California 90012, USA
Tel: (1-213) 617-3300   Fax: (1-213) 617-3399
http://www.omnihotels.com

Opening date: December 1993
Food & beverage facilities: 3
Guest rooms: 371 (including 29 suites)
Contact: Omni Hotels & Resorts

This hotel was built as part of the California Plaza
redevelopment project for downtown Los Angeles,
which includes two high-rise office buildings, the
MOCA contemporary art museum, residential
buildings and the Walt Disney Concert Hall, all of
which are served by modern, high-tech security
systems. Since this grand-deluxe level hotel is
surrounded by numerous fine restaurants, the hotel
itself only has one restaurant and one bar, plus the
Grand Cafe, which serves California cuisine and offers
terrace seating.

The hotel, part of California Plaza, stands seventeen
stories above ground and has two floors below ground.
To the left is a residential building.

Hoku's

The Kahala Hotel & Resort
5000 Kahala Avenue, Honolulu, Hawaii 96816-5498, USA
Tel: (1-808) 739-8888   Fax: (1-808) 739-8800
http://www.lhw.com/ihilani

Opening date: 1963
Renovation date: 1996, 2000
Interior design: Hirsch Bedner & Associates
Food & beverage facilities: 4
Guest rooms: 371 (including 29 suites)
Contact: The Leading Hotels of the World

This hotel was managed by the Hilton when it first opened, then by the Mandarin Oriental hotel group, then in October 2005 it was sold to the current owners and it took its present name. Pacific Rim cuisine was at the peak of its boom in popularity in 1990–95. Hoku's opened in 1996, as a restaurant where diners could enjoy healthy, natural food from Pacific Rim countries. In keeping with Hoku's image the dining room is illuminated in the evening by small lights set in the high, triangular ceiling. Seating is on two different levels, each level decorated to create a different mood, and guests have a choice of seating. The restaurant also offers private rooms for small groups and a small bar at the entrance.

A view of the hotel from poolside. Frames jutting from the exterior support guest-room balconies in this unusual design.
Right: **The main dining room area at Hoku's.**

Cabanas can be rented at the hotel's private beach.
Right page: **Food at Hoku's. Left: Hoku's dessert sampler, the pastry chef's selection of Hoku's desserts (serves two). Right: Five variations of ahi tuna with wasabi cream and ogo daikon salad. Center: Braised beef shoulder with root vegetables and horseradish puree. Back row center: Herb-crusted onaga on creamed spinach with red wine shallots. Back row right: Kiawe-grilled scallops with ginger loi tomato.**

Although Hoku's doesn't advertise itself as a Pacific Rim restaurant, instead billing itself as serving natural food from various Pacific countries, it does in fact serve Pacific Rim cuisine. The restaurant opened in 1996 at the height of the Pacific Rim boom, and on Waikiki there was a glut of restaurants calling themselves Pacific Rim, not all of them living up to the name, so the hotel decided to avoid the tag. There was also the feeling that the high quality of Hoku's would transcend mere Pacific Rim cuisine, popular as it was.

A simple table setting at Hoku's.

The staff at Hoku's.

Azur

JW Marriott Ihilani Resort & Spa at Ko Olina
92-1001 Olani Street, Ko Olina, Hawaii 96707, USA
Tel: (1-808) 679-0079   Fax: (1-808) 679-0080
http://www.marriotthotels.com

Opening date: December 1993
Architects: Killingsworth, Stricher, Lindgren, Wilson & Associates Architects Inc.
Interior design: Gasly Mebery & Associates
Food & beverage facilities: 5
Guest rooms: 387 (including 42 suites)
Contact: Marriott International

This hotel occupies one corner of the huge, 2,600,000-square-meter Ko Olina Resort, which also includes the Ko Olina Golf Course, designed by Ted Robinson, and the Ihilani Spa. The hotel was originally developed and managed by Japan Airlines for six years, but Marriott International purchased it in 1999 and currently manages it. Azur is named after the Cote d'Azur in the south of France, and it has the image of the deep blue sea that that name implies. Next to it is a large bar area.

A view from the beach side.
Right: **The decor of Azur features stately wooden ceilings, plaster walls, wine bottles and various ornaments.**

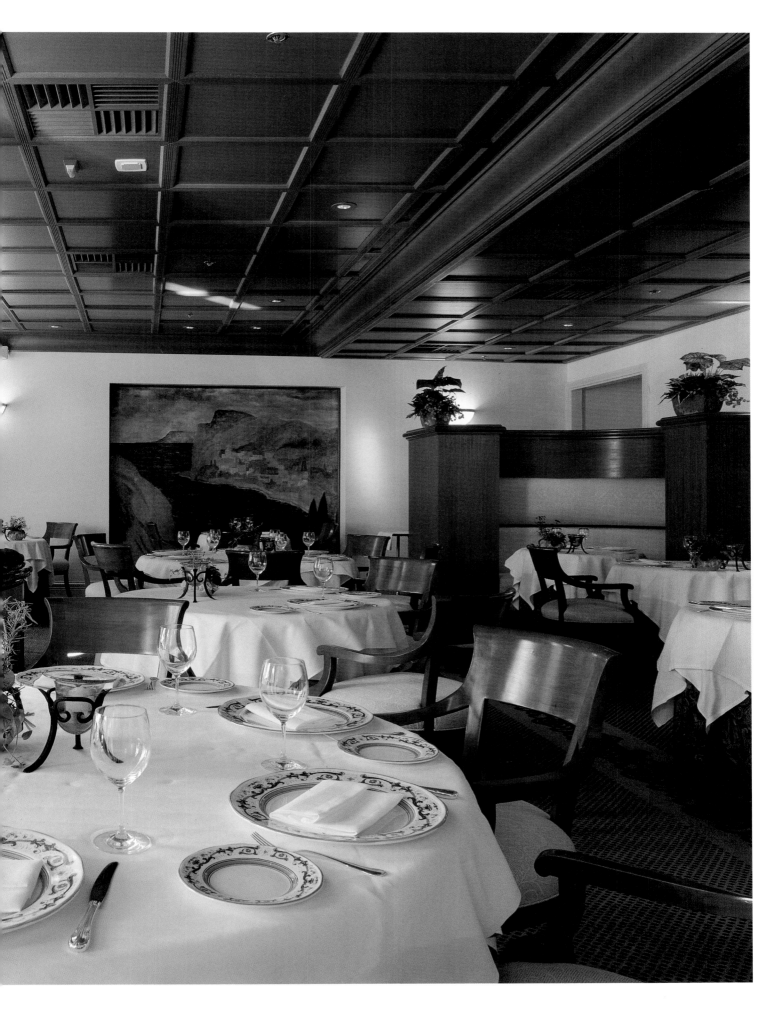

The Prince Court restaurant, with a buffet table on the right and a semi-elliptical dining area to the left.

Prince Court

Hawaii Prince Hotel, Waikiki
100 Holomoana Street, Honolulu, Hawaii 96815, USA
Tel: (1-808) 956-1111   Fax: (1-808) 946-0811
http://www.princeresorthawaii.com

Opening date: August 8, 1991
Architects: Three Architect Ltd., Dallas
Interior design: James Northcut Associates
Food & beverage facilities: 3
Guest rooms: 512 (including 36 suites, 16 villas)
Contact: Prince Hotels, Inc.

A bird's-eye view of the rear of the hotel.
(Courtesy of Hawaii Prince Hotel, Waikiki)

**The hotel is close to
the Ala Moana Shopping Center.**

This is the nucleus of a four-star hotel development in Hawaii by Prince Hotels. The prominent 33-story semi-elliptical twin towers look out over the Ala Wai Yacht Harbor at the western tip of Waikiki Beach. All guest rooms face the sea, and the hotel has adopted an unusual pricing structure where guest rooms on higher floors have a higher room charge. Eleven of the guest rooms are designated as "guest offices" and they provide facilities for carrying out business even while staying at the beach.

The Prince Court is an all-day dining restaurant where guests can enjoy Hawaii's standard cuisine, Pacific Rim. There is a free shuttle bus connecting the hotel with the Hawaii Prince Golf Course on the Waikiki side, and other leisure facilities and shopping areas are nearby.

The Prince Court's semi-elliptical dining
room is decorated in contemporary fashion.
It is located on the second floor of the main
wing between the two towers.

The food at Prince Court. Front row left: Kona prawns
and crab hash. Front row center: Mixed seafood grill.
Front row right: Lobster, scallops and island shrimp
with lobster sauce. Center: Whole island moi fish.
Back row left: Hamachi poke. Back row center: "Fruits of
Summer." Back row right: "Seanna's whim."

The Orchid Court

The Fairmont Orchid, Hawaii
One North Kaniku Drive, Kohala Coast, Hawaii 96743, USA
Tel: (1-808) 885-2000   Fax: (1-808) 885-5778
http://www.fairmont.com

Opening date: August 8, 1990
Architects: Three Architect Ltd., Dallas
Food & beverage facilities: 4
Guest rooms: 539 rooms, 54 suites
Contact: Fairmont Hotels & Resorts

The Fairmont Orchid is located inside the 3200-acre Mauna Lani Resort on the Kohala Coast on the northwest side of Hawaii Island. It was the second hotel to open in the resort, and it was originally called the Ritz-Carlton, after which management was taken over by Starwood Hotels. Then in 2005 management was taken over by Fairmont Hotels. The Orchid Court is a very popular restaurant serving Pacific Rim cuisine with strong French influences.

A view of the hotel's main wing from the lagoon-like pool. The lobby is on the second floor, the cafe is in the basement, and the Orchid Court restaurant is on the second floor of the right-hand building.
Right page: The dining room of the Orchid Court restaurant; there is also terrace seating on the other side of a large door. A uniquely designed chandelier hangs from the pyramid-shaped ceiling.

An aerial view of the hotel; the two ends of the building seem to be reaching towards the beach. The main wing is in the center, with guest-room wings on either side.
(Courtesy of The Fairmont Orchid, Hawaii)

Food at the Orchid Court: Front row left: Apple florentine with fresh fruit. Front row right: Pina goat cheese and grilled vegetable terrine, pistachio vinaigrette. Center row left: Hawaiian vintage chocolate cake with mascarpone mousse. Center row right: Grilled loin of lamb with tropical fruit chutney and crisp potatoes. Top row left: "Seafood trilogy" of pesto-grillled tiger prawn, crab cake, seared ono and ahi. Top row right: Fire-roasted fillet mignon with keahole lobster.

Food at the Coast Grill. Front row left: Coast Grille sampler platter. Front row right: Oyster Bar sampler platter. Center row left: Trio of Hawaiian fish with chef's complementary garnishes. Top row right: Peppercorn-crusted rack of lamb. Back: Four kinds of dessert.

Coast Grille

Hapuna Beach Prince Hotel
62-100 Kauna'oa Drive, Kohala Coast, Hawaii 96743, USA
Tel: (1-808) 880-1111   Fax: (1-808) 880-3112
http://www.princeresorthawaii.com

Opening date: December 1994
Architects: Wimberly, Allison, Ton & Goo
Environment design: Sasaki Environment Design Office
Food & beverage facilities: 5
Guest rooms: 351 (including 36 suites)
Contact: Prince Hotels, Inc.

The famous Mauna Kea Beach Resort on Hawaii Island was originally developed in 1965 by the wealthy American Rockefeller family. In 1988 it was purchased by Seibu Railway Company of Japan, which integrated it with the adjacent Hapuna Golf Course and Hapuna Beach Prince Hotel. The Hapuna Beach Prince Hotel has a unique layout, with dining facilities situated in a six-story open area in the public area at the center of the main wing. Coast Grille, located in a separate wing, has a contemporary interior. The restaurant serves seafood cuisine, and it includes an Oyster Bar where diners can enjoy raw oysters.

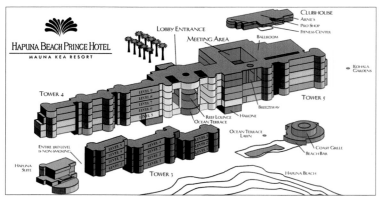

An illustration of a bird's-eye view of the hotel; Coast Grille is located on the second floor of the red building on the lower right.
(Courtesy of Hapuna Beach Prince Hotel)

Right page: **The Coast Grille dining room, on the second floor of a separate building, has a circular plan. A unique feature is the large dome skylight.**

Keka'a Terrace & Dan

Sheraton Maui, Ka'anapari Beach Resort
2605 Ka'anapali Parkway, Lahaina, Maui, Hawaii 96761, USA
Tel: (1-808) 661-0031   Fax: (1-808) 661-0458
http://www.starwoodhotels.com

Opening date: 1963
Renovation date: April 1997
Architects: Wimberly Allison Tong & Goo, Inc.
Interior design: Barry Design Associates, Inc.
Food & beverage facilities: 10
Guest rooms: 133 rooms, 42 suites
Contact: Starwood Hotels and Resorts

This hotel was one of the original buildings built on the northern tip of the Ka'anapali resort area on Maui Island. From January 1995 it was closed for two years while it underwent massive renovation work at the cost of $160 million. The new hotel occupies seven separate buildings on a 23-acre site, and guest rooms have been expanded for a more spacious feel. Also newly built on the cliff overlooking Ka'anapali is the Hale Hoku (House of Stars), a suite-only residential-style wing.

One of the charms of the Keka'a Terrace restaurant has its spacious, resort-style atmosphere. There are a total of ten dining facilities, so that guests won't get bored; these include the Japanese grill restaurant Dan.

Above the pool is a triangular-roofed reception building; Keka'a Terrace is located on the lower floor.
Right: **The open-space Keka'a Terrace features ceiling-high windows reaching the pyramid-shaped ceiling. The site overlooks Keka'a Cape, sacred land on Maui after which the restaurant is named.**

Food at Keka'a Terrace. Bottom row left: potato maki-sushi. Bottom row center: tiramisu. Bottom row right: seared herb-crusted salmon. Top row left: grilled fillet mignon. Top row center: Kanaloa's treasure chest. Top row right: ginger-glazed mocha creme brulee.

Hale Hōkū
(House of the Stars)
Luxury Suites & Rooms

Hale Nalu
(House of the Surf)

Hale Ānuenue
(House of the Rainbow)

Hale Aloha
(House of Welcome)
Lobby

Maui Ballroom

Hale Moana
(House of the Ocean)

Hale 'Ohana
(House of the Family)

Hale Lahaina
(House of Lahaina)

Pu'u Keka'a
(Black Rock Promontory)

Sundowner Bar

Swimming Lagoon

Keka'a Terrace
(Restaurant)

Coral Reef Restaurant
Reef's Edge Lounge

Teppan-Yaki Dan
(Japanese Restaurant)

A bird's-eye view of the hotel grounds.
(Courtesy of Sheraton Maui, Ka'anapari Resort)

Carp swim in the pond at Keka'a Terrace.

A waiting area at Dan.

Japanese grill restaurant Dan has three dining areas and seats 24 persons.

The restaurant's central area viewed from window seats.
Inside the door behind the statue is The Bar, and in
the left-hand corner is the hotel's back entrance.
Right page: **Special features of the window-side seats at Melrose are
the large windows which let in a lot of sun and the high ceilings.
Marble-design plates from Villeroy & Boch are used as presentation plates.**

Melrose

Park Hyatt Washington D.C.
24 & M Street, NW, Washington, D.C. 20037, USA
Tel: (1-202) 789-1234   Fax: (1-202) 419-6795
http://www.hyatt.com

Opening date: 1984
Architects: Skidmore, Owings & Merrill
Interior design: Hirsch Bedner & Associates
Food & beverage facilities: 4
Guest rooms: 225 (including 130 suites)
Contact: Hyatt Hotels & Resorts

The Cafe, which has a fountain on its terrace, is popular with businesspeople.

This hotel in the US capital is one of the Hyatt Corporation's top-level Park Hyatt hotels, which are known for their contemporary feel. The hotels generally have 200-300 guest rooms and numerous restaurants and bars, and they are targeted to business use. Melrose restaurant, the Bar next to it, and the Cafe, which features outdoor terrace seating, are independent facilities designed to meet the needs of busy businesspeople in Washington DC. In addition to the main entrance there is also a back entrance for The Bar and Melrose. They are designed to further the Park Hyatt's image of being a high-class hotel that isn't stiff or formal.

Drapers

The Greenbrier
300 West Main St, White Sulphur Springs,
West Virginia 24985, USA
Tel: (1-304) 536-1110 Fax: (1-304) 536-7834
http://www.greenbrier.com

Opening date: 1858
Reopening date: 1911 (Bath Wing)
Architects: Firm of Harris & Richard
Renovation date: 1950s–1960s
Interior design: Carleton Varney, Dorothy Draper & Company
Food & beverage facilities: 9
Guest rooms: 639 rooms (including 46 suites), 69 cottages
Contact: The hotel directly

When it opened, the Greenbrier was known as a resort hotel that all Americans wanted to experience at least once. In the 1950s it underwent renovation work, and interior designer Dorothy Draper single-handedly created its beautiful interiors. She purchased antique furnishings in the Federalist style that was popular in the early nineteenth century. She also created a unique Greenbrier style, with showy, feminine interiors that lived up to the image of this historic resort. During the 1990 renovation work the hotel created a cafe restaurant called Draper's, which attempted to match the design sense of the late designer.

The facade of the Greenbrier's west wing.
Right: **The resort's symbol, the rhododendron, appears on the ceiling of Draper's restaurant.**

The Gotham Bar & Lounge

The Peninsula, New York
700 Fifth Avenue at 55th Street, New York, NY 10019, USA
Tel: (1-212) 956-2888 Fax: (1-212) 903-3943
http://www.peninsula.com

Opening date: 1905
Architects: Higs & Weeks
Renovation date: 1998, 2004
Interior design: Hirsch Bedner & Associates
Food & beverage facilities: 3
Guest rooms: 185 rooms, 54 suites
Contact: The Peninsula Hotels

The Gotham Hotel, built at a cost of $2.25 million, opened on Fifth Avenue nearly a century ago, with nineteen floors and 400 guest rooms equipped with bathrooms and providing butler service. It has an Italian Renaissance flavor, with a design based on the Beaux Arts style that was popular in that era. In October 1989 it was purchased by the Hong Kong-based Hongkong and Shanghai Hotels, Ltd. for $127 million, and it was renamed after the company's famous Peninsula Hotel in Hong Kong. Guest rooms were completely renovated between 1998 and 2004. The Gotham Bar and Lounge serves afternoon tea in the style of the Peninsula in Hong Kong; cocktails are available in the evenings.

The hotel's Fifth Avenue facade. In 1998 a spa opened on the top three floors.
Right: The Gotham Bar and Lounge serves afternoon tea. There is a bar in the front corner.

Riingo has a mezzanine-level private dining room called Riingo's Mezzanine.

Riingo

The Alex
205 East 45th Streeet at third Avenue, New York, NY 10017, USA
Tel: (1-212) 867-5100   Fax: (1-212) 867-7878
http://www.lhw.com/alex

Opening date: March 2004
Architects: Costas Kondylis & Associates
Interior design: David Rockwell, the Rockwell Group
Food & beverage facilities: 2
Guest rooms: 70 rooms, 130 suites
Contact: The Leading Hotels of the World

This contemporary apartment hotel is located just two minutes from Manhattan's Grand Central Station. Riingo restaurant, with its sushi bar, is earning a reputation in New York's Japanese-restaurant world. Riingo and Riingo Cafe and Bar are not managed by the hotel, but are under the control of a specialized restaurant management company, which provides the chefs and restaurant floor staff. This style is perhaps a notable trend in 21st-century hotel food operations systems.

A view of the 33-story hotel from the revolving-door entrance.
Right page: **Riingo's contemporary interior. What appear to be candles are actually images projected onto the walls by projectors.**

Riingo's chef, Johan Svensson; there is also a sushi counter.

Central Park South seen from Asiate.
Right page: **Asiate, with small private dining rooms on the left and right. The decorative lighting fixtures on the ceiling were custom made.**

Asiate

Mandarin Oriental New York
80 Columbus Circle at 60th Street, New York, NY 10023, USA
Tel: (1-212) 805-8800   Fax: (1-212) 805-8888
http://www.mandarinoriental.com

Opening date: December 2003
Architects: Brennan Beer Gorman Architects, L.L.P.
Interior design (food and beverage facilities): Tony Chi
Interior design: Hirsch Bedner & Associates
Food & beverage facilities: 3
Guest rooms: 149 rooms, 52 suites
Contact: Mandarin Oriental Hotel Group

This popular new restaurant, located on the twenty-first floor of an eighty-story building overlooking Central Park, is currently one of the most talked-about restaurants in Manhattan. The interior was done by the Asian-born designer Tony Chi, who lives in New York, and it has an Asian-influenced contemporary feel. There is currently a boom in health-conscious Japanese cuisine in Manhattan, and the restaurant has employed a French-trained Japanese chef. His style of "French-Japanese" cuisine is making a strong impression, and the restaurant is so popular that it's hard to get reservations.

The restaurant is located on a middle floor on the right side in the twin buildings of the Time Warner Center.

A bottle rack in the restaurant's entrance.

**Asiate's chef, Noriyuki Sugie, and his cuisine.
Left: king crab with asparagus and cucumber.
Held by the chef: roast chicken breast,
Indonesian curry-spiced confit chicken legs,
ginger-scallion chutney, smoked foie gras
and celery puree.**
Right page: **From Asiate diners can see a row of
seven hotels along Manhattan's hotel row on
Central Park South.**

**Etuvee of abalone, mixed seafood yuzu ceviche,
surf clam salad, pickled vegetables.**

**Chocolate fondant with raspberry compote,
mascarpone ice cream, raspberry yuzu granite.**

Rotunda

The Pierre, New York—A Taj Hotel
Fifth Avenue at 61 Street, New York, NY 10021, USA
Tel: (1-212) 838-8000   Fax: (1-212) 940-8109
http://www.lhw.com/pierre

Opening date: 1930
Architects: Schultz & Weaver
Renovation date: 1992
Interior design: Bradshaw & DePalma, New York
Food & beverage facilities: 3
Guest rooms: 149 rooms, 52 suites, 75 residences
Contact: The Leading Hotels of the World

The Pierre Hotel stands at the eastern edge of Central Park South in Manhattan. Rotunda, serving breakfast, light lunch and cocktails, is a unique New York institution that has been open since 1968. One special feature is its 360-degree panoramic wall murals that extend to the ceiling. The design is fashioned after the image of an arbor in an open-air courtyard in a mansion belonging to an aristocratic family in Italy. The paintings are the work of Edward Melcarth (1914–1973), who was known as a painter, sculptor, teacher and writer and was born in Louisville, Kentucky. He studied in London, in Paris, and at Harvard University in America, and he had a deep appreciation of Italian Renaissance painting. Here in the Rotunda he used the techniques of contemporary Renaissance painting and trompe l'oeil painting, with subject matter ranging from mythical gods and contemporary celebrities to his own pet cat, Sacha.

A view of the 42-story hotel from the small park at the eastern end of Central Park West where the statue of General Sherman is located. The hotel has a Georgian-style facade.
Right: **The Rotunda is known among long-term New York residents for its afternoon tea.**

Afternoon tea at the Rotunda. Fifteen different teas are available, including Japanese sencha green tea.

The mural also includes trompe l'oeil pillars.

This is said to be a portrait of former US first lady Jacqueline Kennedy and her two young children.

The sea god Neptune, there is also a portrait of the goddess Venus.
Right page: **A view of Rotunda from the stairway; the front door is the entrance to the banquet facilities.**

Next Spread: **The ceiling of Rotunda is painted with trompe l'oeil sky and clouds.**

Profile

Hiro Kishikawa

Photo-journalist

Hiro Kishikawa was born in 1951 in Otaru City on Hokkaido, Japan. After traveling about 50 countries of the world as a movie cameraman for FIS World Cup Ski Races and WRC (World Rally Championship), in 1982 he switched to a photo-journalist and specialized in photographing some 400 first-class hotels around the world as his life's work. He is a regular contributor to several magazines such as *Traveller* (Conde Nast), *The Gold* (JCB Card) and *Impression* (Amex).

Main works for the advertising media: Hino Motors' calendar in 1987 *Windows of the World* that won a prize in a Japanese nation-wide calendar competition, Renault's advertisement *1999 LUTECIA*, Fuji Film's brochure *1998, 2000, PHOTO-KINA*, and many others.

Main published works: *Great Hotels of the World* and *Classic Hotels of the World*— each 6 volume photograph collections with bilingual texts, published by Kawade Shobo Shinsha. These books can be bought at bookstores of many countries and at Web sites of Amazon.com, Barnes & Noble, Yahoo, and so on.

http://www.kplann.com (Hotel Maniac Era)
hiro@kplann.com
Contact: **KEI. PLANNING**
Tel: 03-3408-0288
Fax: 03-3478-3552

Noboru Kawazoe

Architectural Critic

Born in 1926 in Tokyo, Japan, Mr. Noboru Kawazoe graduated from Department of Architecture, Waseda University. After the chief editor (1953–57) of the magazine "Shinkenchiku" (New Architecture), he became an architectural critic and organized "Group Metabolism" with architects and designers in 1959. While serving as member of Japanese executive committee of World Design Conference (1960), sub-producer of Expo Osaka's theme-pavilions (1969), visiting professor of Waseda University (1993–96), he founded the think tank CDI in Kyoto in 1970 and Japan Society of Lifology in 1972. He is now the representative of CDI.

Mr. Kawazoe was received Mainichi Publication Culture Awards in 1960 by his book *Dwellings of Gods and the People*, Kon Wajiro Award in 1982 by *Proposal of the Lifology*, and Minakata Kumagusu Award in 1997.

Main published works: *What is Design?* (Kadokawa Shoten), *Dwellings of Gods and the People* (Kobunsha), *Proposal of the Lifology* (Domes Shuppan), *Kon Wajiro* (Chikuma Shobo), and many other books.